W9-DCN-576

Unsafe Haven

Unsafe Haven

**The United States, The IRA
and Political Prisoners**

Karen McElrath

Pluto Press

LONDON • STERLING, VIRGINIA

First published 2000 by Pluto Press
345 Archway Road, London N6 5AA
and 22883 Quicksilver Drive,
Sterling, VA 20166–2012, USA

British Library Cataloguing in Publication Data
A catalogue record for this book is available from
the British Library

ISBN 0 7453 1322 1 hbk

Library of Congress Cataloging in Publication Data
McElrath, Karen, 1959–
   Unsafe haven : the United States, the IRA, and political prisoners /
      Karen McElrath. p. cm.
   Includes bibliographical references and index.
   ISBN 0–7453–1322–1
      1. United States—Relations—Great Britain. 2. Great Britain—
Relations—United States. 3. United States—Foreign relations—1993–
4. United States—Emigration and immigration—History—20th
century. 5. Northern Ireland—Emigration and immigration—
History—20th century. 6. Irish Republican Army. 7. Political
prisoners—Legal status, laws, etc.—United States. 8. Deportation—
United States. 9. Extradition—United States. I. Title

E183.8.G7 M37 2000
303.48'273041—dc21   99–046659

Designed and produced for Pluto Press by
Chase Production Services, Chadlington, OX7 3LN
Typeset from disk by Stanford DTP Services, Northampton
Printed in the EU by TJ International, Padstow

Contents

Acknowledgements

I am grateful to a number of people in the United States and in Ireland who have assisted with this book. I am indebted to those persons who agreed to be interviewed, in particular the prisoners and former prisoners. Thank you for your trust and for sharing some of your experiences and insights with me. Several people assisted me with establishing contacts. Mike Duffy was instrumental in the early stages of the research. His efforts in disseminating information for and encouraging the 'Writing Campaign' are acknowledged. The collection by Francie Broderick and others provided a good basic summary of a number of cases, very much needed in the early stages of the project. Tim Cotton provided me with considerable information – a researcher's dream. I thank you. Bill McClellan of the *St. Louis Dispatch* writes with both interest and integrity. Thank you for your articles. Thanks to Jackie Dana and Eugene McElroy whose services kept me informed of Irish issues east and west of the Atlantic. John Knowles of the Law Library, Queen's University, was most helpful as were staff at the Linen Hall Library, in Belfast. Thanks to Bob Connolly, who provided me with copies of his books, and to Kirk Olson for granting permission to use his lyrics both here and for a previous article. Family members and friends in the United States and in Ireland were very supportive and I am grateful for your assistance and inspiring words. Finally, to Anne Beech at Pluto Press, your patience was truly appreciated. Thank you very much.

Karen McElrath
Queen's University
Belfast

To A. R. M.

Foreword

Karen McElrath has addressed an important facet of 'The Troubles': the treatment of Irish political prisoners in America. The prisoners issue has always been a central one in republican theology. On the one hand there is the constant IRA concern: 'Break the lads in prison, and you break the movement.' On the other, the disputed question of legitimacy, out of which the present Sinn Féin party emerged via the hunger strikes. Those hunger strikes and Mrs Thatcher's contribution to 'ten men dead' were the contemporary equivalent of 1916. The ten men died to show that the IRA thought of themselves not as criminals but as prisoners of war.

One man's freedom fighter has always been another man's terrorist and as the war in Northern Ireland intensified, so did the propaganda war intensify worldwide. Much of the media coverage took the view that the IRA were terrorists simpliciter. However in the key arena of American public opinion, the Irish American quotient (43 million, according to the 1990 census) was not disposed to accept this construct uncritically. A factor not understood either in Dublin or London throughout the 1970s and 1980s was the re-awakening of a consciousness of being Irish amongst a steadily increasing segment of that 43 million, and a parallel shaping of that consciousness by, with or from the Northern Ireland troubles.

People could and did put their heads up over the parapet on issues like the MacBride principles and on getting the Carter administration to check the flow of arms to the RUC. However, despite the Carter administration's concern for human rights issues and a fact finding visit to the Six Counties in 1978 by two members of Congress, which found 'serious violations' of human rights, the State Department's human rights report for that year made no reference to

Northern Ireland. The institutional force of the 'special relationship' between London and Washington meant that
increasingly, to the Irish American activists to be staffed by
British Foreign personnel with American accents. Neither was
the Justice Department en rapport with the activists. It
unleashed the FBI on Republican fugitives.

However the Carter administration, not surprisingly in
view of the strong Irish component of the Democratic Party,
was generally sympathetic to Irish nationalism. But Carter's
crocuses of the Clinton spring time were killed off by the long
winter of the Reagan/Thatcher love-in conducted with
orgasmic rapport in economic, political and military
boudoirs. McElrath chronicles how, after Thatcher had
permitted US bombers to engage Gaddafi's camels from
British air bases, the Murdoch press duly struck up a chorus of
'You owe us one', under the energetic baton of Attila the Hun.

The debt of gratitude was duly paid. Reagan changed the
law which admitted of a political offence exemption for
fugitive Irish republicans. Extradition warrants fell thick and
fast as a result.

The emergence of the Clinton candidacy and of a new
dynamism amongst the young Irish Americans, who had first
been mobilised over the issue of increasing the allocation of
visas to the Irish, led to the Peace Process. Without the White
House there would have been no Good Friday Agreement, no
IRA ceasefire. Another result was a considerable thaw in the
American Administration's approach to the question of Irish
political prisoners. I doubt very much whether, at the time of
writing, many of the miscarriages of justice which Karen
McElrath details would occur in the present climate.

However, the Peace Process could break down at any
moment and the figure of the IRA prisoner fighting
extradition in American Courts could very well once more
become a focus for agitation, fund-raising and heartache
both at a personal level, and at the level of the relationships
between Dublin, London and Washington.

McElrath's work is therefore both timely and instructive.
From my own experience of giving evidence in IRA trials in
London, Paris and New York I would have to say that in
either Paris or New York the attitude of the courts is light

years in advance of that which obtains at the Old Bailey. One may argue if one wishes that Irish bombs do not go off in either France or America. But the factual position is that in the French and American capitals, the atmosphere of the court is simply that of dealing with a legal problem: should the defendant be regarded as a political offender entitled to asylum, or should he be considered a criminal terrorist, and extradited back to England or Northern Ireland? Whereas in England even an expert witness walks into an atmosphere of hostility.

I was involved in two of the most celebrated American cases, that of Joe Doherty and, in 1998, the most recent court proceedings concerning Charlie Caulfield. In the Caulfield case, the jury found that Caulfield could remain in the United States, even though he had entered a negative to the emigration question inquiring whether he had any criminal convictions.

Caulfield's lawyer, Mike Dowd, mounted the successful defence that a young man standing in Green Street courthouse in the dock where Robert Emmet once appeared could not in conscience have regarded his sentence as proceeding from criminal activity. No, he was following in the footsteps of a long line of Irish patriots. That defence would hardly have sufficed under Ronald Reagan and it would have been laughed out of court, and probably cost Caulfield a few extra years for good measure, had it been mounted in London. The sight of an Irish republican in an English dock is one calculated to revive all the old xenophobia and anti-Irish prejudice of Shire Tory England.

The American Republican tradition, in the Jefferson/Paine sense, and the fact that so much of that 43 million's heritage derives from the Famine and successive revolutionary waves of emigration, has created a different climate.

In that climate, very respectable people who have no sympathy for terrorism nor any particular affection for the IRA, nevertheless, either because of a knowledge of the defendant's character, or out of a sense of abstract justice, will lobby and contribute financially to the very expensive legal challenges mounted to the deportation of Irish Republicans from America.

But climate or no, cases of gross injustice can and have occurred, as McElrath's detailed treatment of, for example, the Francis Gildernew, Liam Ryan, and Matt Morrison cases shows. The power of the British lobby in Washington was not to be underestimated. In the Brian Pearson case, Judge Williams granted Pearson asylum, saying that his offence, an attack on a barracks in Northern Ireland, was a 'political' event. However, pro-British elements in the Justice Department promptly secured an appeal against the decision.

But probably the best, or worst, example was that of the most famous Republican prisoner of all, Joseph Doherty. Initially, a New York judge accepted the arguments of myself, and the late Sean MacBride, that Doherty's actions were politically motivated, and he won his case. However, nine years of subsequent legal battles followed, during which Doherty remained in jail. He was finally sent back to Northern Ireland to serve out his sentence. His offence had been involvement in the shooting of an SAS officer, Captain Westmacott, compounded by subsequently escaping from jail and fleeing to America, where his case became a *cause célèbre*.

A New York Street was called after him. He was named as Honorary Grand Marshal of the St Patrick's Day Parade, and Cardinal O'Connor visited him in jail. However, *cause célèbre* or no, when Doherty was returned to Belfast, he was given no credit for the time served in American jails, and was serving his full 20-year sentence when the Good Friday prisoner releases came. By contrast, McElrath cites the case of Peter McMullen, 'Peter the Para' as he became known to the IRA, after he began to co-operate with security forces.

McMullen had actually bombed paratroop barracks, and not surprisingly, after the British succeeded in having him extradited from America, he was sentenced to fourteen years at York Crown Court in 1996. However, the judge took the years he had spent in prison into consideration and McMullen walked free.

Another glaring contrast to Doherty's treatment was that of Orlando Bosch, who was jailed on several charges of attacking Castro's personnel and economic targets, including attacks on ships. However, powerful anti-Castro elements in

Miami successfully lobbied Washington decision takers to have Bosch released.

No lobbying would be of any use in the case of John McIntyre, who was murdered in Boston, presumably by Republican sympathisers, after being set up as an informer in the affair of the Valhalla arms shipment. This appeared at first simply to be an attempt to smuggle arms into Ireland via a trawler which rendezvoused with the Valhalla off the Kerry coast. It now emerges, from many sources, including researches of my own for my forthcoming book on the Irish diaspora, that John McIntyre was the innocent victim of a labrynthine plot in which the FBI were involved, but which was allowed to go ahead as a sting operation to discredit the IRA.

These fascinating, albeit disturbing, individual cases apart, the overall subject which McElrath has chosen is, as I said at the outset, a highly important one. In a nutshell it illuminates how, the much vaunted American Constitution notwithstanding, British diplomacy succeeded in making the American court system an arm of its counter-insurgency effort in Ireland. This fact may yet be shown to hold more than merely historical relevance should the Peace Process break down. I commend this book.

Tim Pat Coogan

Introduction

For at least 150 years the United States served as a 'safe haven' for persons of Irish descent who, in their quest for Irish independence, participated in politically-motivated behaviours. Some individuals fled Ireland to avoid what they perceived to be unjust prosecution. Others escaped from British-controlled prisons. Additionally, at various times throughout history, persons of Irish descent and other supporters of Irish independence in the United States provided assistance in the form of funds, weaponry and other supportive mechanisms to fellow patriots in Ireland. In response to these actions, about which the US government had ample knowledge, more often than not legal intervention was not initiated by the US government. This 'hands off' policy continued for years until the 1970s when US law enforcement under the direction of the executive branch began to target Irish republicans for the first time in US history. Since the change in policy commenced, the United States can no longer be viewed as a venue of refuge.

Historically, non-intervention represented the standard practice for dealing with Irish republicans in the United States as well as the acceptable US presidential policy in relation to the Irish conflict. In the twentieth century, the strategy of non-intervention into the Irish conflict by the US executive branch was based largely on its relationship with Britain. In a reciprocal manner, the strategy also contributed to the strengthening of the US–Britain alliance. This book examines these issues.

Chapter 1 provides an abridged description of the history of Irish republicans in the United States – the reasons for their arrival, the welcome they received and, in some instances, the success that they achieved in that country. Britain considered several of these persons to be fugitives of justice, common criminals in need of severe punishment and sanction. Indeed, high treason carried the punishment of death. This chapter also provides historical illustrations of the US presidential policies as they related to the Irish conflict. The examples serve to highlight the US–Britain relationship in this regard.

Chapter 2 focuses on several issues relating to the deportation of Irish Republicans from the United States. Although the United States has been described as a nation of immigrants,[1] immigration policies have often targeted various ethnic groups for harassment or exclusion (American Civil Liberties Union 1996). Until recently the United States provided informal refuge to Irish republicans who had been convicted of politically-motivated offences in Ireland. This policy changed in the 1970s and since that time a number of Irish republicans have faced immigration controls or deportation from the United States. The change reflects a growing trend by the United States government in which immigration decisions are often based on foreign policy considerations. For example, persons who have immigrated to the United States 'from countries officially regarded as "democratic" are less likely to be granted political asylum[2] than persons who enter from "communist" countries' (American Civil Liberties Union 1996, p. 4). Because the United States officially regards Britain as a democratic nation (United States Department of State 1996, p. 1), it follows that persons from the north of Ireland who seek political asylum in the United States will be denied this refuge; granting asylum would indicate that persons were victims of past persecution and so would suggest that the United States' greatest ally engages in human rights violations which are inconsistent with democratic principles.

In a number of cases, deportation proceedings commence after the Immigration and Naturalization Service (INS), a branch of the Justice Department, claims that persons failed to disclose past criminal convictions in the north of Ireland. Official INS forms request whether persons were convicted in their 'country of origin' for a 'crime of moral turpitude'. For ideological reasons, Irish republicans differentiate between 'crime' and politically-motivated behaviour that resulted in conviction in the north of Ireland. Thus when US officials ask whether the person has been convicted of a crime, the rational response is 'no'. In other cases, Irish republicans refuse to acknowledge the conviction or any other legal proceeding against them in the north of Ireland, arguing that the proceedings were biased in favour of the prosecution (that is, on behalf of the British government).

Extradition represents another tool for excluding persons from the United States. Extradition is the legal process by which one state requests of another that a person be returned for trial or punishment. Procedures are guided by extradition treaties between two states. Chapter 3 examines extradition issues relating to Irish republicans in the United States. Relevant cases are reviewed and the effects of the US–Britain alliance are highlighted. Some of the individuals who have faced extradition hearings in the United States escaped from Long Kesh prison[3] in the north of Ireland in 1983 and settled in the United States where they were arrested in the 1990s. Even if extradition is denied, these persons will still face deportation for entering the United States illegally. The tools of extradition and deportation are compatible in that they share the same goal, that is, to exclude 'undesirables' from US borders and other ports of entry.

The focus of Chapter 4 is on Irish republicans who have been convicted in the United States for offences relating to their political beliefs, namely the transporting or conspiring to transport arms or other weaponry for use by the Irish republican movement. Irish Nationals in this group who have been convicted in the United States, generally face deportation proceedings upon their release from prison. At one US federal prison site, the deportation facility is located nearby, ready and waiting so as to hasten the journey home. US-born or naturalised citizens have been imprisoned for illegal weaponry transactions, although their citizenship protects them from deportation.

Chapter 5 includes a discussion of the role of the US media in reporting the Irish conflict, which is influenced heavily by the British perspective. Media portrayals of the 'Irish problem' are important in that they have the potential for shaping public opinion and policy. Mainstream media in the United States have for the most part practised selective reporting, in which important background and contextual material is omitted.

US President Bill Clinton has been credited by various people for helping to bring 'peace' to Northern Ireland. Indeed, he has demonstrated his committed interest in this area, far more so than any of his predecessors. Chapter 6 describes several of Clinton's policies regarding the north of Ireland. Information is presented that suggests that Clinton's policies in this regard are both shaped by and affect the special relationship between the United States and Britain.

The shift in US policy towards Irish republicans occurred in the 1970s and onwards. The concluding section suggests explanations for the change. It is argued that the change in policy was influenced by several factors, including the reciprocal dependency and support extended between the United States and Britain in war and various military operations. The impact and ideology of the Provisional IRA and how that ideology was portrayed by the British government also contributed to the policy change.

Terrorism

In the opening pages of Celmer's book on terrorism, he referred to the United Kingdom as one of the '...most victimised nations' of terrorism (1987, p. 1). The meaning of terrorism, however, is both subjective and selective, and 'used to describe violence of which the user disapproves' (Miller 1994, p. 6). Definitions of terrorism depend on a host of factors, including the victim, the target, the reason for the act, the ideology of the actors and the background and interests of the definer. With respect to Northern Ireland, terrorism, specifically IRA violence, is viewed by many writers (for example, Kingston 1995) as a threat to British democracy. In fact terrorism is portrayed as the true and only threat to democracy in this region of the world. Democracy, however, should not be perceived in simple dichotomous terms; governments cannot be divided into the limited categories of 'democratic' and 'undemocratic' nations. Democracy should be viewed on a spectrum whereby relevant governments can be categorised by the extent to which basic democratic principles are applied equally to all people. In some instances, governments that fail to employ democratic principles equally, can in effect create 'terrorism'. Also, official as well as common usage of the term generally fails to include violence, intimidation or terror tactics by the State. Also, official usage of the term, when defined by governments, generally fails to include state-sponsored aggression, intimidation or other terror tactics.

This book is based in part on my interpretation of the experiences of Irish republicans who have faced deportation, extradition or prosecution in the United States. These individuals have rejected the label 'terrorist' and because this book seeks to highlight their experiences, the use of the word is inappropriate. Additionally, recognising the subjectivity of the term in the north of Ireland and elsewhere, I tend to avoid it.

Irish America

The 'Irish Diaspora' is a concept used much more widely in Ireland than in the United States. Conversely, the phrase 'Irish America' is used in both places, but definitional problems and stereotypes surrounding the phrase abound. Irish America has been described as an 'abstract concept' (O'Hanlon 1998a), and so it is. People use the term, however, as if it describes some homogeneous group in terms of its culture, shared beliefs and values. With some writers the term has been used in a more restrictive manner, referring to Americans of Irish descent who share a sense of historical and contemporary events as they pertain to Northern Ireland. Many Irish Americans, perhaps even a majority, have little knowledge or interest in the conflict in the north (Hayden 1998) and this indifference dates back to at least the early 1900s (Miller 1985). Thus, although millions of Americans claim Irish descent, very few would be considered to be part of what Arthur (1991, p. 145) referred to as the '*active* Irish diaspora'. A number of Irish Americans have little knowledge or interest in the Irish conflict perhaps because they assimilated into America a long time ago and thus are culturally and physically distanced from Ireland. Further, most Irish Americans have no experience of being victimised in their lifetime by colonial rule for any extended period of time and, also, their 'whiteness' prohibits them from identifying with an oppressed group.

To equate Irish republican supporters in the United States with Irish Americans is to miss the mark, for the latter includes people who simply do not give a damn about the Irish conflict and the former includes persons who don't have a drop of Irish blood in their genealogical past. I am reminded of the Jewish woman of Italian descent who is an active member of Irish Northern Aid in a northeastern state and of the various Irish issues for which African Americans have voiced their concern in support of Irish nationalists. Those are but two examples of several Irish republican supporters who have no (immediately known) blood ties to Ireland.

Some have argued that knowledge of the Irish conflict has increased among Irish Americans in recent years and that 'improved journalistic coverage' is one explanation for the change (Shannon 1993, p. 12). 'Coverage' may indeed be more substantial than in past years but the extent to which that coverage adequately represents the events in the north remains to be seen (see Chapter 5).[4]

With regards to the term 'Irish America', initially I had attempted to avoid it altogether but this practice became too difficult in some sections. Therefore I too have fallen victim to its usage, although recognising the limitations of the concept.

1

History

'Scratch a convict or a pauper, and the chances are that you tickle the skin of an Irish Catholic.' Chicago Post, *Editorial, 1869. Quoted in Farquhar (1999)*

In the eighteenth and nineteenth centuries several Irish Nationals who engaged in politically-motivated behaviour for Irish independence sought and found refuge in the United States. The 1798 Alien Act, which coincided with the rebellion in Ireland, authorised the US President to deport persons whom he considered to be dangerous, but the Act was not executed and expired within a few years. Few immigration controls were enforced between 1790 and 1875, except during the period of massive immigration that occurred during the Great Hunger (Irish Famine) when US authorities directed ships to quarantine areas in their efforts to confine disease-stricken passengers.

Historically, the executive branch of the US government chose a policy of 'non-intervention' with regards to the Irish conflict. Various US presidents viewed the 'Irish Question' as a domestic matter to be settled by Britain (and later by both Britain and Ireland). To do otherwise would risk the very nature of the US–British alliance. The practice of non-intervention has been heralded by US presidents who have suggested that it is unwise to interfere with the internal affairs of another country. Neutrality is the best approach in these matters they have argued. Failing to intervene, however, supports the status quo in the north of Ireland. Equally important, this policy has sent a powerful message to the British government that has served to justify its presence in all or part of Ireland. Thus, a policy of non-intervention has worked to support, if not encourage, the British presence in Ireland and has also strengthened the alliance between the two governments.

This chapter provides a brief historical background of Irish political dissidents in the United States as well as US government policies regarding these persons. Additionally, illustrations of the non-intervention policy with respect to the Irish conflict are highlighted.

Safe Haven

In the nineteenth and early twentieth centuries, many Irish persons arrived in the United States after escaping from British prisons. During this period extradition treaties between the United States and Britain (enacted in 1794 and 1842) made no mention of political offences, yet in no instance did the United States agree to extradite Irish political offenders. Between 1794 and 1842 the executive branch, rather than the judiciary, was responsible for extradition decisions (Bassiouni 1974) but various US presidents were committed to protecting political offenders. This allegiance was voiced by President Tyler who stated publicly that persons would not be extradited for engaging in revolutions for liberty.

In 1848, several members of the Young Ireland[1] movement fled to the United States after warrants had been issued for their arrest in Ireland. Most were wanted for treason and faced the penalty of death by British authorities. John Blake Dillon and Michael Doheny were charged with treason but not apprehended, having managed to escape to the United States. Dillon was admitted to the New York Bar in 1849 (O'Cathaoir 1990). Richard O'Gorman, another escapee, also prospered in law in New York and later became a state appellate court judge (Miller and Wagner 1994). Paradoxically, both men had been charged with treason by British officials, a crime that carried a maximum punishment of death in Ireland and the only crime worthy of mention in the US constitution.

Some members of the Young Ireland movement were convicted of treason and sentenced to transportation rather than death as the British did not wish to produce martyrs (O'Cathaoir 1990). John Dillon arranged to meet President

Fillmore personally to discuss the Irish political prisoners. Fillmore, however, refused to intervene on the prisoners' behalf (Cronin 1987; O'Cathaoir 1990) but nor did he or others press for extradition or deportation when Terence MacManus, Thomas Francis Meagher and John O'Mahony arrived in the United States in the 1850s after escaping from British custody in Van Diemen's Land (now Tasmania). In contrast the men were given a hero's welcome upon their arrival in the United States. MacManus ventured to San Francisco in 1851 and people rejoiced '...in every Irish centre of influence throughout the United States' (Keneally 1998, p. 241).

John Mitchel, another Young Irelander convicted of treason, was transported to Bermuda and later to Van Diemen's Land, from where he escaped to the United States in 1853. Later he advocated slavery and subsequently fought for the Confederacy in the US Civil War. Mitchel's views were thus contradictory; '[Mitchel] was inspired not by love of liberty but by hatred of England' (Woodham-Smith 1962, p. 417), and despite a history of strong opposition, both Mitchel and the British actively supported the southern states during the US Civil War. Thomas Francis Meagher held the leadership position of General in the Union Army. Thus, Mitchel's ally in Ireland had become his enemy in America during the US Civil War.[2]

James Stephens and O'Donovan Rossa founded the Irish Revolutionary Brotherhood[3] (IRB) in Dublin in 1858. In the same year, John O'Mahony and Michael Doheny founded the Fenian Brotherhood, the United States affiliate to the IRB (Metress 1995). The Fenian Brotherhood was organised in order to provide weaponry, army officers and, at times, volunteers (Ó Broin 1971). Within six years the Fenian Brotherhood consisted of approximately 10,000 men and subsequent recruitment drew thousands more (Kee 1972). During this time, Stephens escaped from Richmond Prison in Dublin and arrived in New York, where he was welcomed 'by a massive gathering...[and a] watchful press' (Cronin 1971, p. 100). The Fenians, a term coined by John O'Mahony, openly purchased various weaponry in the United States for use in Ireland. In 1865 the US Secretary of State provided passive support for the organisation's methods in that he did not condemn their actions, largely because relations between the United States and Britain at the time were weak (Wilson 1995). One year later, the republican movement in the United States reportedly raised $500,000 for the purchase of weaponry for Irish rebels (Tansill 1957). In later years, Clan na Gael,[4] an Irish-American group whose members supported an Irish republican ideology, financed the Fenian Ram, a sea vessel designed for attack on the British Navy (Wilson 1995). During the Boer War (1899–1902), Clan na Gael supported the Boers and publicly criticised the behind-the-scenes alliance between the United States and Britain. At one point, members and affiliates of the united Irish societies in Chicago fought with the Boers under the auspices of a Red Cross delegation, with funding provided by the Ancient Order of Hibernians (Tansill 1957).

John Devoy, imprisoned in Dublin for five years, came to the United States in 1871 after amnesty was granted for several prisoners. He was an early leader in Clan na Gael, and also helped to orchestrate the fundraising for the rescue of Irish political prisoners held in Australia (MacUileagóid 1996; O'Rourke 1993).[5] This escape venture succeeded and neither Devoy nor the ship's crew were charged with a crime. Moreover, the endeavour brought considerable respect for Clan na Gael (Miller 1985).

Dynamite attacks in England in the 1880s were financed by Clan na Gael and persons engaged in the attacks sought refuge in the United States (O'Grady 1976). One proposed treaty sought to extradite persons who had used dynamite against British targets, despite having political reasons for using this form of weaponry. After lengthy debate, the US Senate refused to incorporate the 'dynamite clause' and a political offence exception was included when the new treaty was signed in 1889 (Farrell 1985). This extradition treaty provided judges with legal justification for denying extradition requests for persons whose activities were politically motivated. By the late nineteenth century, Britain became so concerned with Irish America that it requested British agents to infiltrate American groups that supported a republican ideology (Norton-Taylor 1997).

Persons of Irish descent accused or convicted of politically-motivated offences in Ireland or in England continued to visit or find refuge in the United States during the latter part of the nineteenth century. Their arrival occurred despite the US immigration law, passed in 1875, which prohibited 'convicts' (and prostitutes) from entering the United States. For instance, Thomas Clarke came to New York in 1898 and although a former prisoner he was granted US citizenship in 1905 (he later returned to Ireland where he was executed in 1916). The political offence exception to extradition was exercised in 1903 when proceedings were held against James Lynchehaun who had been convicted in Ireland for the attempted murder of a female landowner. He later escaped from prison and settled in the United States. A defence committee was formed in his name and its members rallied for political asylum. Tansill (1957) characterised the US State Department as 'anglophile' during this time; however, the judiciary agreed that the attempted murder constituted a political offence, thus, Lynchehaun was not extradited.

John Boyle O'Reilly arrived in the United States in 1869 after escaping from prison in Australia. He later became a 'celebrated newspaper publisher' in the United States (MacUileagóid 1996, p. 38). Patrick McCarten, a member of the Supreme Council of the Irish Republican Brotherhood escaped from British authorities and arrived in the United States in 1917 (O'Rourke 1993). Eamon de Valera visited the United States between 1919 and 1920 during which time he raised $5,000,000 (O'Rourke 1993; Wilson 1995) through a bond campaign despite having escaped from Lincoln Jail in England just prior to his arrival. In fact, his execution by the British in 1916 may have been prevented largely because he was a US citizen.[6] His mother (in New York) and wife (in Ireland) obtained a copy of his birth certificate, '...as proof that he could claim the protection of American citizenship' (Coogan 1993, p. 78).[7] Although refuge was provided to Irish political offenders during this period, the alliance between the United States and Britain was strengthening, and thereby reducing any possibility that the US government would provide support for Irish independence.

In the 1920s, Ireland issued to the United States a number of extradition requests yet no arrests were made (Farrell 1985). This practice of granting refuge to Irish republicans continued for decades. Irish republicans who sought refuge in the United States in the 1940s and 1950s also faced no threat of deportation. In fact, some INS (Immigration and Naturalization Service) officials at the time discussed with these persons their previous convictions for political offences and also their role in the Irish Republican Army. In one case, a staff person with the INS was aware of these acts but he stated to the applicant that it was not necessary to record those types of offences on the application (personal communication with applicant, 1995). The US government certainly had the means by which to identify Irish republicans. During this time visa applications were screened by a special board composed of members from the Federal Bureau of Investigation (FBI), INS, the US Department of State and US military intelligence. The board was established in 1941 in the interests of promoting greater security (Divine 1957). Irish republicans, some of whom entered the US during this time, were not judged to be 'security risks'.

The historical evidence indicates that Irish political dissidents did not face deportation or extradition from the United States largely because the executive branch made no significant attempts to exclude these persons from seeking refuge in the United States. Nor was there any proactive legislative attempt to alter the recognition of a political offence exception. At the same time, however, the executive branch did little to facilitate Irish independence; rather the official US policy was one of non-intervention.

Non-Intervention by the Executive Branch

The special relationship between Britain and the United States was established around 1900 albeit weakly (Ward 1968) but even before that time the US government was at best lackadaisical about Irish affairs. For example, during the Irish Famine[8] *government* intervention from the United States was minimal and largely irrelevant. In some instances the US government ceased to collect transportation tolls on donated cargo supplies bound for Ireland (Woodham-Smith 1962, p. 242) and permitted two US ships, previously used for war, to transport food and supplies to Ireland (Gallagher 1994, p. 79; Woodham-Smith 1962, pp. 243–5). In 1847, the Vice-President of the United States attended a public meeting in Washington, D.C., the outcome of which was to encourage local meetings nation-wide for the purpose of raising funds for Irish relief (Woodham-Smith 1962, p. 241). In the same year, however, congressional legislation known as the Passenger Acts raised ship fares from Ireland to the United States for the purpose of reducing the number of impoverished Irish who were fleeing starvation and disease (Woodham-Smith 1962, p. 239).

The vast majority of relief, however, came not from the US government but from funds collected locally. The Quakers were instrumental in this regard as were Catholic churches, Jewish synagogues, various native American groups and Irish-born Americans. But food and supplies shipped from the United States and from elsewhere could not halt the starvation. For many Irish persons, emigration was the only means of survival. The Passenger Acts, however, made it difficult for many of the Irish to purchase fares to the United States. Moreover, ships were turned away from US ports and were often forced to land at Canadian sites. These measures suggest that the US government was willing to provide some relief to the Irish as long as 'the problem' remained in Ireland. Similar reactions characterised the US populace whose views of the Irish changed from the 'unfortunate victims' [the Irish in Ireland] to the 'scourings of Europe' [the Irish Hunger emigrants in the United States] (Woodham-Smith 1962, p. 248). Four decades later Irish immigrants in America were still viewed with repulsion, and portrayed by many as ' 'faery' folk, or as barbaric apes' (Kincheloe 1999, pp. 41–2).

Since 1900 relations between the United States and Britain have varied in strength but the alliance has never disappeared altogether (Dobson 1995). The alliance between the two governments has been described as a 'special relationship' whereby the US government has for the most part sided with its British ally on issues relating to the Irish conflict. President Woodrow Wilson, for example, whose term in office (1913–1921) provided an opportunity to assist Ireland in its quest for independence, failed to do so largely because of his close alliance with Britain. He was dependent on Britain for its support for the League of Nations and although Wilson argued for the right to self-determination for all people (Dobson 1995), he appeared to have applied this belief selectively.

Some have suggested that Wilson disliked Irish Americans because of his own bigotry and also because he questioned their loyalty (Metress 1995). Wilson's alliance with Britain, his sympathy for Protestants in the north of Ireland[9] (Johnson 1980) and his heritage – his mother was English (Handlin 1990) – contributed to his refusal to intervene in the execution of Roger Casement. In this refusal, Wilson argued that intervention on his part would result in 'international embarrassment' (Tansill 1957, p. 210). Support for Casement was extended by the US Senate whose members requested clemency for Irish political prisoners. Under suspicious circumstances, however, the congressional plea did not reach British authorities until after Casement had been executed (Cronin 1987). Some have argued that the reason for the delay rested solely with the President (Hartley 1987; Tansill 1957). Prior to the Easter Rising, John Devoy had communicated in writing with German officials in Berlin informing them of the date on which the Rising would occur. That correspondence was seized by the US Secret Service in a raid of the New York offices of the German Counsel General and subsequently provided to the British Embassy by the State Department (Tansill 1957). Following the Easter Rising approximately 2,000 republicans from Ireland were imprisoned in England and Wales. Later that year, and continuing through until June 1917, the prisoners were released, at which time most returned to Ireland where they were granted amnesty by the British Prime Minister (RM Distribution 1999).

President Warren Harding, who served immediately after Wilson (1921–1923), saw no distinction between political and ordinary crime. If in fact a difference existed, he reasoned that political offenders should be treated more harshly than other non-political offenders because the former sought to erode the basic American institutions. Given the views of Presidents Wilson and Harding, it is not surprising that a US-manufactured ship was sold to the British who used it for imprisonment during the 1922 internment period in the north of Ireland (MacUileagóid 1996). It is likely that in many ways the executive branch influenced this transaction, and by doing so, provided support to the British presence and rule in Ireland.

Beginning in 1939 and continuing throughout the Second World War, relations were strong between President Franklin Roosevelt and Winston Churchill, First Lord of the Admiralty and later Prime Minister. It was Churchill who first used the term 'special relationship' to describe the alliance between Britain and the United States. President Roosevelt was critical of the south of Ireland for its commitment to neutrality during the Second World War. Under his administration US troops were stationed in the north of Ireland to assist the allies, but without the consent of Dublin (Cronin 1987). However, during Roosevelt's leadership, Frank Aiken, former Chief of Staff of the IRA, visited the United States for a series of public speaking engagements in several cities, returning again in 1948 with de Valera (Coogan 1993).

With encouragement from the US State Department, President Truman, who served from 1945 to 1953, failed to respond at all to a document that contained thousands of signatures from America, asking for assistance to end partition (O'Clery 1996a).

In 1951 the US House of Representatives debated the issue of a resolution that would call for an end to partition but the measure was defeated. A confidential memorandum issued by the British embassy in Washington, D.C. indicated that the south of Ireland's commitment to neutrality was one reason for the resolution's defeat (Arthur 1991).

John F. Kennedy was recognised as the first Irish American Catholic to hold the office of president. He visited the south of Ireland just months before he was assassinated but never ventured north of the border. Despite his ethnic background he avoided any official discussion about partition and was viewed by the Irish as being 'pro-British' (O'Hanlon 1998b).[10]

During President Nixon's term (1969–1974), the INS implemented its 'Lookout System', whereby persons entering the United States were screened for associations with terrorist activities (Celmer 1987). Also during the Nixon administra-

tion and shortly after Bloody Sunday,[11] Ireland's Foreign
Minister visited Washington, D.C. and pleaded for assistance:
'We would hope that these friendly nations would turn
Britain away from the lunatic policies she is pursuing...We
regard what has been done as an act of war' (quoted in
Cronin 1987, p. 304). The United States Secretary of State,
however, refused to intervene (Cronin 1987). During this
time, Britain supported US interventions in Vietnam and the
official US policy regarding Irish republicans began to change
dramatically. For the first time in history, US law
enforcement began actively to target supporters of the Irish
republican movement (see Chapter 4). During the administrations of both Presidents Nixon and Ford, various law
enforcement sectors in the United States participated in
efforts to locate, use surveillance on, and investigate IRA
supporters in that country (Clark 1977).

In the 1970s, US Senators Daniel Patrick Moynihan (New
York) and Edward Kennedy (Massachusetts), House Speaker
Tip O'Neill and Governor Hugh Carey (New York), collectively known as the 'Four Horsemen', denounced the IRA and
urged Americans to cease providing funds to organisations
that supported the IRA. They later formed the 'Friends of
Ireland' which also comprised a number of congressional
members. Legislative debate in the United States had surfaced
regarding the legal status of the Ulster Defence Association
(UDA) in Northern Ireland. In the early 1980s, the 'Friends of
Ireland' postponed a resolution in Congress that would have
called for the end of the UDA's legal status.

In 1979, Lord Mountbatten was killed with three others by
an IRA bomb. The device had been planted on his boat and
exploded as he, family members and friends sailed the
Sligo/Donegal coast. On the same day, 18 soldiers were killed
when an IRA bomb exploded in the army barracks in
Warrenpoint, County Down. These events angered the
British a great deal, and some have argued that it was this
that caused the United States to succumb to British pressure
and begin to target US supporters of the Irish republican
movement (Adams 1986).

A US ambassador to the south of Ireland once described President Carter's policies on Northern Ireland as 'neutral but not indifferent' (Shannon 1993). Carter promised that he would continue the tradition of the executive branch and exercise impartiality with regards to Northern Ireland. Indeed the Secretary of State under the Carter Administration noted that, 'For us to intrude ourselves into the Irish Question would not be wise. I think it would be resented by the parties concerned' (in Hartley 1987, p. 198). To be neutral or impartial on issues relating to Northern Ireland, however, in effect implies a support for the status quo. To his credit, President Carter was the first president to pledge support for job investment in the north (O'Brien 1995). Under his administration, however, and with approval from the US State Department, a manufacturer in the United States had sold various weaponry to the RUC for their use. Carter allegedly stopped the sale of weapons, a decision influenced greatly by the congressional Ad Hoc Committee on Irish Affairs, which indicated that the weaponry transactions violated Carter's policy that prohibited weapon sales to countries with a record of gross violations of human rights (Guelke 1984). Carter is often credited with the termination of official weapon transactions for the RUC, however, after Carter's term in office ended, the sale was 'still under review' by the US Department of State (Cronin 1987, p. 317).[12] At the time Britain had access to other sources of weaponry, including its own manufacturers, but a sale authorised by the United States would have cemented the partnership – silent or otherwise (personal communication with Sean Cronin, October 1996).

Carter, then, appeared to be more willing to risk the US–Britain alliance. However, since 1972 and continuing throughout the Carter Administration, congressional hearings on Northern Ireland were banned. In 1978 during Carter's term in office, two members of Congress conducted a site visit to the north of Ireland. Upon their return to the United States they sent a letter to President Carter informing him of 'reports of serious violations of human rights being experienced by the people of Northern Ireland' and noting that:

The people of Northern Ireland are being subjected to warrantless searches and arrests, prolonged detention without charges, harsh interrogation methods, and non-jury trials in which a single judge sits alone imposing long-term sentences (Eilberg and Fish 1979, pp. 213–14).

The delegates informed President Carter that they had been 'appalled' by their observations in Northern Ireland (Eilberg and Fish 1979, p. 214). Despite this communication, the State Department's 'human rights' report for that year made no mention at all of the north of Ireland (Holland 1999). Douglas Bennett, Carter's Assistant Secretary for Congressional Relations, responded to the congressional members on behalf of President Carter. Bennett reported that Carter acknowledged the Administration's concerns about 'alleged events in Northern Ireland' but that 'means exist to check these allegations' (Eilberg and Fish 1979, p. 217). The 'means' to which Bennett referred included British-based committees. Moreover, the Carter Administration noted its great faith in the British government in the area of human rights: 'The British Government states it will not condone the ill-treatment of persons held in [police] custody...' (Eilberg and Fish 1979, p. 217). Efforts directed at Irish republicans in the United States began to intensify under President Carter. For example, the 'PIRA Squad', a code name for an FBI operation that targeted IRA suspects, was in full operation during this time (Taylor 1997).

The developing relationship between President Ronald Reagan and British Prime Minister Margaret Thatcher contributed greatly to the intensity of the focus on Irish former political prisoners in the United States. At no time in United States history was the special relationship stronger than when Reagan and Thatcher were in power. They were united in their definitions of threatening as well as friendly governments. They corresponded and met often, holding 15 Anglo-American summits, the greatest number of such meetings held by any previous US President (Dobson 1995). They were also personal friends. Although Reagan encouraged Thatcher to develop ties with the south of

Ireland, with regards to the north he chose not to intervene (O'Hanlon 1998b).

Early in his term, considerable international concern emerged over the impending deaths of the hunger strikers. By 13 July 1981 six republican prisoners, fighting for political prisoner status, had died on hunger strike. At that time the Irish government issued a request to Reagan asking him to apply pressure on Margaret Thatcher for a resolution. Like his predecessors, however, President Reagan refused to intervene.

In 1983 a US Senate committee proposed that the government appoint a special envoy to identify ways to assist the British and Irish governments in obtaining peace in the north of Ireland. The State Department flatly refused the rec-ommendation noting that '...a special envoy would serve no useful purpose...' (O'Clery 1996a, p. 10, 29). That same year the State Department was allowed to implement its Anti-Terrorism Assistance Program, designed to provide US-based counter-terrorism training to representatives from US allies (Celmer 1987).

Summary

Historically, the executive branch of the US government has viewed the 'Irish problem' as one best handled by Britain: non-intervention has been the standard procedure with respect to this issue. The policy of non-intervention is symbolic in that by failing to act or apply pressure or condemn, British policies are both supported and legitimised by the United States.

Foreign intervention can be viewed in terms of degrees with condemnation at one end of the spectrum and military occupation at the other. Condemnation, for example, represents a less intense form of foreign intervention, a publicly-stated opinion in the aftermath of some event. It is uncertain whether US intervention into the Irish conflict would have altered history in any way. If President Wilson had requested clemency for the 1916 rebels, would they have been sentenced to prison rather than executed? If Nixon had condemned the actions of the British paratroopers in the

Derry massacre, would it have made any difference with respect to the context of the official inquiry or to the prosecutions of the military personnel involved? During the 1981 hunger strikes Ronald Reagan was perhaps one of the few foreign leaders who was in a position to influence Margaret Thatcher. If he had intervened and asked for compromise at least, would the ten martyrs have died? These questions are speculative, the answers unknown. It is possible, however, that US intervention into these events at the very least might have altered, temporarily or otherwise, the US–Britain alliance in the years that followed.

In spite of the policy of non-intervention by the executive branch, throughout most of the nineteenth and twentieth centuries political prisoners from Ireland were not targeted by the US government for exclusion. Deportation and extradition, common tools used to exclude 'undesirables' from US borders and ports of entry, were not used against this group. Changes in official policy, however, were soon to come.

2

Deportation and Other Immigration Controls

'Let no Irishman, then, imagine that by fighting for his country he commits a crime. He commits a crime, on the contrary, by not doing so...' *Thomas Davis, Essay on the Morality of War, in Sillard (1908, p. 135)*

'Violence where there is an alternative is immoral, but violence where there is no alternative is survival.' *Testimony by Brian Pearson, political asylum hearing, March, 1997*

'[The British government] obviously rejects the idea that an act of violence is political. No one in Northern Ireland is in prison...for their political beliefs.' *Robert Chatterton-Dixon, British Embassy (Washington, D.C.) Spokesperson, commenting on the political asylum decision in Brian Pearson's case, in Willing (1997)*

People use various methods to enter the United States illegally. Some individuals enter under false identities and with false documents, whereas others enter with factual names but fail to disclose past convictions (Hutchinson 1981). Still others enter legally but remain in the United States beyond the permitted time period. Persons can be deported for any of these reasons. At times, however, the Immigration and Naturalization Service (INS) uses its discretionary authority and allows people to remain in the United States despite their having entered the country illegally. In this instance, deportation proceedings are not initiated by the INS.

This chapter provides a brief historical overview of US immigration controls. Refugee policy and political asylum are described with special reference to Irish former political prisoners. This chapter also includes descriptions of selected deportation cases that have involved Irish republicans in the United States.

US Immigration Policies

In the past two decades several Irish former political prisoners have faced deportation or other immigration controls (for example, the denial of visitor visas) for their past convictions in British courts. Attempting to exclude former political prisoners from the United States represents a significant change in US policy, for never before in history has the US government targeted such persons. The shift in policy commenced in the early 1980s and strengthened throughout that decade, reflecting the US–Britain alliance whereby Margaret Thatcher established not only a close friendship with Ronald Reagan but was also influential in shaping US foreign policy (Dobson 1995).

It is possible that stricter US immigration controls and greater use of deportation against Irish republicans has been influenced by anti-immigrant sentiment that characterised much of the US populace during the 1980s. This argument, however, fails to recognise that anti-immigrant feeling has a long and established tradition in the United States and has in fact been part of the social fabric of that culture throughout history. The concept of the 'dangerous alien' which emerged in the early 1900s led to 'mass deportations' (Allen 1974, p. 56; Schrecker 1996–1997). For at least 150 years anti-immigrant sentiment in the United States was accompanied by changes in immigration policies whereby reasons for excluding certain groups were based on individual attributes or country of origin, policies which often reflected stereotypical attitudes and bigotry on the part of policy makers.[1]

Persons excluded by US immigration law according to their individual status have included prostitutes (1875) although exclusion was not used against persons seeking their services, the illiterate (1917), the mentally 'defective' (1907), the diseased (1910), the poor (1910), and communists (1950), alleged or otherwise. In the early twentieth century, categories for exclusion represented 'friendless, despised, ignorant, defenseless people, and, more important, *unorganized*' [emphasis in the original] (Preston 1963, p. 19).

Immigrants entering from certain counties were favoured more than others. For example, persons entering from northwest Europe were more likely to be admitted to the United States than were persons from southern Europe and this practice continued until the late twentieth century. This type of immigration control, for example, by country of origin, was established in the early 1900s when quotas for entry were developed based on the ethnic composition of the United States, that is, the number of persons permitted to enter from any one country was based on the percentage of the persons from that country who were already residing in the United States. The greater the number of US citizens within the particular ethnic group, the greater the number of persons admitted from that country. Under that system, persons from Britain represented the highest percentage of immigrants who were permitted to enter the United States. Critics argued that the quota system was discriminatory in that it favoured immigrants from Britain and the entry quota was eventually revised after research showed that the method used to classify persons of 'English' descent was flawed (Divine 1957). However, the national origins quota system continued well into the twentieth century and was repealed in the 1960s when immigration policy began to focus more on family reunification.

'Foreign convicts' or persons convicted of 'crimes involving moral turpitude' in other countries, have been denied entry into the United States since the late nineteenth century. Confusion surfaced over what behaviour constituted a crime of moral turpitude. In 1908, an attorney with the US Department of Labor defined it as behaviour 'activated by malice...so far contrary to the...moral sense of the community, that the offender is brought into public disgrace' (cited in Preston 1963, p. 248). The category included both felonies and misdemeanours.

Congressional legislation, however, did not intend that political offences should be considered crimes of moral turpitude (Preston 1963). Persons convicted of political offences were viewed differently from 'criminals' in that the former were permitted to enter and remain in the United States. This safeguard was a fundamental part of immigration policies enacted in 1875, 1882, 1891, 1901, 1903, 1907, 1910, 1917, and 1952, all of which excluded persons convicted of criminal offences but admitted persons whose offences were political (Hutchinson 1981). Moreover, persons who had entered the United States through misrepresentation (e.g. an alias) were permitted to remain if they were able to convince authorities that they feared persecution if they returned to the home country. This discretionary practice continues today.

In the early twentieth century, deportation was used extensively to prohibit 'dangerous' foreign nationals from remaining in the United States (Allen 1974, p. 56). As a tool for exclusion, deportation can also be used against persons whose activities threaten the interests of US allies. For example, in 1987 eight US residents (most of whom were Jordanian) were arrested on immigration offences that actually stemmed from their distribution of pro-Palestinian literature (Deutsch and Susler 1991). The individuals were 'connected to' the Popular Front for the Liberation of Palestine. During deportation hearings a judge found that the INS had 'targeted' the individuals for their political activities, in violation of the First Amendment of the US Constitution. The US government appealed but the appellate court's ruling supported the claim of the eight individuals. Further appeal by the government was made to the US Supreme Court. In what has been termed 'a depressing performance' by *New York Times* journalist Anthony Lewis (1999), the high court ruled that the INS decision to seek deportation based on the individuals' political views was *not* in violation of the First Amendment.

In other cases, deportation has been used as a threat to coerce people to provide information. Ridgeway and Farrelly (1994) described the experience of Kevin Corrigan, an Irishman who resided in New York. In 1990 he was threatened with deportation by the Federal Bureau of Investigation (FBI); he could remain in New York, agents promised, if he were willing to provide information about certain persons who frequented area bars. Agents also reminded Corrigan of Liam Ryan, a naturalised US citizen who was murdered after he returned to Ireland. Corrigan was approached a second time, by FBI agents in the company of a Special Branch officer from the RUC. He again refused to inform and left the United States shortly thereafter.

Visitor Visas

Applications for a visitor or tourist visa must be approved by the US Department of State. If granted, persons are permitted to enter and remain in the United States for a specified period of time. Persons who overstay the permitted period are subject to deportation. The State Department's decisions in granting visitor or tourist visas are also politicised. Between 1989 and 1990, the United States granted tourist visas to hundreds of Cubans but failed to prosecute those who overstayed (Domínguez 1992). In the 1970s and early 1980s, the State Department policy towards Irish republicans was greatly restricted in that several former prisoners were denied visitor visas (Wilson 1995). The introduction of this visa policy coincided with the most recent commitment of British troops that commenced in 1969. Through various interviews conducted in the 1970s, two members of the US Congress discovered that the State Department screened visa applications of Irish nationals by utilising 'lookout cards', that contained information on '*suspected* Provisional IRA members' [emphasis added] (Eilberg and Fish 1978, p. 3). Staff affiliated with the US Embassy in London and with the US Consul General in Belfast reported using local newspapers to screen for convictions. The credibility of both methods is questionable. Eilberg and Fish (1979) found that that some Irish Nationals who had been denied visas had never been convicted; rather, simple detention without charge was used as an explanation to deny visas in some cases. The congressional members also found that the visa policy in the 1970s appeared to be biased against Irish republicans, several of whom had applied for visas but were denied them. For others, such as Joe Cahill and Ruairi O'Bradaigh, then President of Sinn Féin, multiple entry visas had been issued by the State Department only to be revoked later. Eilberg and Fish noted that reasons for denial and revocation were unclear. In 1975, after Cahill and O'Bradaigh had their visas revoked, several loyalists were granted visas by the State Department. Three were members of the Ulster Volunteer Force, an illegal paramilitary group.

In 1996 the State Department denied visas to Brian Campbell, Laurence McKeown and Felim O'Hagan, editors of a book (Campbell et al. 1994) that featured several accounts from persons who were imprisoned at Long Kesh during the 1980–81 hunger strikes. The three editors had been asked by the prestigious World Affairs Council to present a lecture in northern California (*Irish Echo* 1996, p. 4) – and all three were former political prisoners in the north of Ireland.

The State Department does permit visitor visas for Irish former prisoners when it is advantageous for them to do so. Since 1971 veteran republican Joe Cahill had been prohibited from entering the United States. Cahill was a respected leader in the republican movement and the best candidate for clarifying the issues regarding the planned ceasefire to supporters in the United States (O'Clery 1996a). With encouragement from Jean Kennedy Smith, Ambassador to the south of Ireland and former Taoiseach Albert Reynolds, who believed that Irish republican support from the United States was critical, President Clinton directed the State Department to issue the visitor visa. In 1999 Cahill was again granted a visitor visa and spoke in various US locales.

In 1997 the State Department granted a three-week visitor visa to Sean O'Callaghan, former IRA volunteer turned paid informant for MI6 who on several occasions publicly renounced violence and condemned the IRA from his prison cell and upon his release. His visit to the United States was sponsored by the (London) *Sunday Times* (Adams 1997). Initial reports suggested that he was scheduled to testify for the prosecution in Brian Pearson's deportation case (Millar 1997; Pearson's case is discussed below). That strategy changed, however, perhaps as a result of the negative publicity that surrounded his visit in the United States.

Refugees and Foreign Policy

Refugees are persons who have fled political or religious persecution but in the United States, and perhaps elsewhere, the degree of persecution, indeed its very existence, is first determined by the US government. The executive branch uses the criterion 'special humanitarian concerns', to define groups within each world region. Individuals from within each group must first establish persecution or a well-founded fear of persecution on account of race, religion, nationality, membership in a particular social group or political opinion. This criterion, outlined in the 1980 Refugee Act,[2] is consistent with the definition provided by the United Nations Convention Relating to the Status of Refugees and its 1967 Protocol. Individuals must then meet one or more 'preferences' decided upon by the executive branch (for example, facing life-threatening danger; seeking reunification with immediate family members). In sum, refugee status is determined first by the group to which one 'belongs', and second by the individual's personal experience.

In most instances, the Department of State decides refugee status and this determination is made largely on the basis of how the State Department views the extent of political persecution in the country of origin (Schoultz 1992). In theory, the State Department considers the number of political prisoners, the presence of death squads and other important indicators of persecution. But these indicators are not defined for the public. For example, it is not known how the State Department differentiates between 'political' and 'non-political' prisoners, or how it estimates the number of political prisoners in a particular country. The term 'death squad' is also undefined. Further, it is not known whether definitions of these terms are applied equally across countries, regardless of the relationships between the United States and foreign governments.

The Refugee Act of 1953 provided assistance to persons escaping from communist countries only, and since that time refugee status has been linked with foreign policy issues. Persons from Northern Ireland who fear persecution have yet to be officially recognised as 'refugees' by a US administration. The strong and obligatory alliance between the United States and Britain affects this decision; refugee status generally is not given to those persons who flee 'friendly regimes' (Zolberg 1990, p. 112). Guidelines for establishing refugee status specify that the *source* of persecution is not restricted to government officials in the home country; rather, persecution from non-government sources in the home country can also lead to the designation of refugee status, particularly if the government does not or cannot protect them. Throughout history various ethnic interest groups have pressured the executive branch and this influence has led to the designation of refugee status for members of that particular group. It is precisely this type of influence that is needed if refugee status is ever to be granted to persons who flee political and religious persecution from the north of Ireland. A number of Irish Americans, however, lack the interest or understanding of the Irish conflict so that widespread pressure on the executive branch has not been forthcoming.

Political Asylum

Legal definitions differ for refugees and asylum seekers; refugees are not physically present in the United States at the time of application. Persons who arrive in the United States (legally or illegally) may request political asylum if they are 'unable or unwilling to return [to the country of origin] because of a well-founded fear of persecution' (Schoultz 1992, p. 202). This standard 'fear of persecution' draws from inter-national conventions relating to both political asylum and refuge. If asylum is granted, persons may apply for United States permanent residency after one year (permanent residency can also be granted without a request for political asylum). In theory, successful bids for asylum are determined by the INS, although in practice the INS does not act inde-pendently; rather, the Bureau of Democracy, Human Rights, and Labor (formerly the Bureau of Human Rights and Humanitarian Affairs), a division of the US State Department, reviews each application for political asylum and advises the

INS district director or the immigration judge (Dietrich 1988). Although the opinion of the State Department is not binding in asylum applications, its decision is weighed heavily by the district director or judge. In one study, INS officers in New York reported that opinions [of the State Department] are always followed whether the State Department recommendation is positive or negative (Fagen 1984). According to its own *Country Reports on Human Rights Practices: The United Kingdom*, the US Department of State views Britain as a democratic nation (1997a, p. 1; 1996, p. 1). As a consequence, the Department is unlikely to find that asylum applicants from the north of Ireland have a fear of persecution. Schoultz (1992, p. 204) argues that the role of the State Department in asylum decisions represents an area 'where sizeable doses of U.S. foreign policy are injected into U.S. immigration policy' and that phrases such as a 'well-founded fear of persecution' are vague, which contributes to biased interpretations, consciously or otherwise. Irish former political prisoners upon their release from prisons in Northern Ireland at times fear for their safety. Fear is generated not only from the actions and threats by loyalist paramilitaries but also from state agents (for example: police, British Army) of social control. The US government fails to acknowledge the legitimacy of these fears. To do otherwise would risk the alliance with Britain.

Approval rates for political asylum differ substantially depending on applicants' country of origin; successful bids for asylum depend on US foreign relations. The Commissioner of the Immigration and Naturalization Service, Doris Meissner, has acknowledged this link: 'Because the United States was supporting the government of El Salvador, a low percentage of asylum grants served US foreign policy objectives' (Meissner 1988, p. 63). In 1983, applicants from Nicaragua were four times as likely (9.5 per cent) as applicants from El Salvador (2.4 per cent) to be granted asylum (Maranz 1984). In fact nearly all Salvadorans were denied political asylum during the 1980s, a time when that government was viewed as 'friendly' by the United States (Mitchell 1992). The advent of a communist government was followed by an increase in successful bids for political asylum among Nicaraguans. In 1987, 35 per cent of Nicaraguans were approved for political asylum and in 1988 that figure nearly doubled, reaching 68 per cent. In sum, country differences in political asylum rates are best explained by foreign policy interests (Schoultz 1992) and political asylum applicants from countries whose governments are allies with the US are disadvantaged (Gerety 1988; Mitchell 1992).

It is useful to compare US immigration controls directed against Irish republicans with those applied to Cubans, thousands of whom were permitted to enter the United States shortly after the Cuban government identified with a Marxist-Leninist ideology in 1961. Significant and proactive efforts on the part of the United States were introduced in 1965 when an 'airlift' designed to transport immigrants from Cuba to the United States was funded by the US government (Domínguez 1992). The 'freedom flights' lasted seven years, during which time thousands of Cubans, including political prisoners, were permitted to enter the United States. Large numbers of Cubans came to the United States from Mariel Bay shortly after the 1980 Refugee Act was passed. President Carter refused to categorise them officially as 'refugees' but in 1984 President Reagan adjusted the status to lawful permanent residency for the majority of these Cubans immigrants. During two decades of Cuban immigration, Domínguez (1992) estimated that fewer than 50 per cent of the Cubans who entered the United States would have been able to show a well-founded fear of persecution.

Recent Struggles for Refuge: Selected Cases

In recent years, the US government has demonstrated its eagerness to deport Irish former political prisoners. Proactive efforts to deport Irish republicans from the United States commenced largely in the late 1970s and the early 1980s.[3] In many instances deportation proceedings were linked with foreign policy objectives in that the relationship between the United States and Britain determined the treatment of individuals who sought entry into the United States.

Michael O'Rourke

In 1975, Michael O'Rourke was convicted and imprisoned in the south of Ireland for possession of illegal firearms and explosives. He escaped from prison in 1976 and subsequently entered the United States. He was arrested in 1979 for illegal entry into the United States, at which time he was asked to leave the country voluntarily. He refused, deciding instead to fight deportation and arguing that his actions were political.

At the time of his arrest in 1979 there was no extradition treaty between the United States and the south of Ireland; the south could not issue an extradition warrant to the United States. O'Rourke acknowledged his involvement in the IRA to US authorities and this information was used against him in several decisions. He was denied bail and remained in INS custody from 1980 to 1984. Never before had a 'deportee' been incarcerated by the INS for that length of time.[4] INS and the Bureau of Immigration Appeals (BIA) acknowledged that '...Mr. O'Rourke's presence in this country would be detrimental to relations between the United States and both Ireland and Great Britain' (United States Senate 1984, p. 2). Despite the concern raised by the INS and the BIA, the case was not likely to affect foreign relations with the south of Ireland. Joseph Roche, the former president of the (US) Ancient Order of Hibernians, testified before a Senate Sub-Committee that the Taoiseach (then Charles Haughey) had informed Roche that the Irish government was 'not interested in having O'Rourke returned' (United States Senate 1984, p. 42). Similar reports were voiced by a senior member of the Irish parliament (Connolly 1985). The US government was much more interested in maintaining and strengthening its relationship with Britain than with the south of Ireland.

The administrative judge initially appointed to the case testified before a US Senate Sub-Committee that, based upon the evidence, he would have granted permanent residency to O'Rourke but that he had stepped down from the case because he had been harassed and intimidated by the INS (United States Senate 1984). At one point he had been followed by INS agents from the court to his home, a distance of 125 miles. He testified that other immigration judges had also been harassed by INS district directors. A second judge was appointed, but O'Rourke's attorney testified that the second judge had a reputation for siding with the government and that the judge had been 'handpicked' (United States Senate 1984, p. 38). Indeed in 1983 the second judge ruled against O'Rourke, denying him adjustment of status and political asylum and denying the request to withhold deportation. The United States Supreme Court refused to hear the case and O'Rourke was deported to the south of Ireland shortly thereafter. By that time he had been imprisoned for nearly five years in US jails.

Francis Gildernew

In Dungannon, County Tyrone, housing shortages in the 1960s created significant problems, particularly for Catholic families whose requests for houses were often delayed in favour of Protestants (McCluskey 1989). The Gildernew family from East Tyrone were actively involved in this issue and in the civil rights movement in Northern Ireland overall. Intimidation was commonplace and attacks on the family were frequent; the family home had been fired upon and a bomb had been placed underneath the vehicle of a family member. At one point the family fled to the south of Ireland.

By the time he was 23 years old, Francis Gildernew had been arrested without warrant on at least ten occasions, although no charges had been filed on those occasions. He was arrested in England when he was 23 and subjected to intensive interrogation. He then signed a 'prepared' confession citing his involvement in the placement of a landmine and his membership in the IRA. He was tried and convicted in a Diplock court.[5] He has always argued his innocence.

Francis Gildernew served eight years in Long Kesh and was released in 1984. He arrived in the United States on a visitor visa shortly thereafter. He subsequently met Sharon and the two were married in 1985. Poughkeepsie, New York is not known for its Irish community. It is a small city located on the Hudson River, north of New York City. It is here that the couple lived peacefully, where they owned and operated an Irish pub.

Francis Gildernew had been granted permanent residency and was well on his way to becoming a US citizen. In 1991, however, after residency had been granted, the Gildernews learned of the possibility that immigration proceedings might commence when they were refused a second liquor licence and further, that the current licence was facing revocation because of pending deportation proceedings. In 1992 over half a dozen agents from the FBI and the INS entered the Gildernew home, guns drawn. Francis was placed in shackles, arrested and charged with fraud in his application for a green card on which he had denied being imprisoned for a 'crime of moral turpitude'. Gildernew perceived that he had answered that question truthfully.

After Francis' arrest, a judge set a bail amount and within one day of his arrest, the small community had donated $10,000 towards bail. Gildernew's supporter and friend, Tim Cotton reported that most of the donors had never met Francis Gildernew.

In 1991–92 Gildernew had actively promoted passage of New York State legislation that incorporated the MacBride Principles,[6] a set of guidelines that promote employment equality in US corporations based in Northern Ireland. The impetus for the legislation included historical and contemporary data that showed patterns of employment discrimination against Catholics in the north. The British government has vehemently opposed the MacBride Principles and has made several attempts to hinder the passage of this legislation in the United States (see, for example, McManus 1993; O'Neill 1995b for claims that Britain opposed MacBride legislation in California). An estimated $5,000,000 dollars has been spent by the British government in their efforts to thwart MacBride legislation. Other estimates have been more than twice that amount (O'Hanlon 1998b). Gildernew's role in the successful passage of MacBride in New York appeared to have contributed to his arrest. On 24 July 1992, United States Representative Hamilton Fish wrote to the INS District Director William Slattery: '…[it] appears our government arrested [Francis

Gildernew] solely because of his prominent advocacy of the adoption of the MacBride Principles legislation by the State of New York'.[7] Several members of the US House of Representatives discussed the relationship between the United States and Britain in connection with the arrest of Gildernew (Cotton 1994). For example, US Congressman Joseph P. Kennedy[8] stated:

> It is widely believed that [Francis Gildernew] is coming under fire from this Administration for exercising his constitutionally protected right of free speech for trying to win passage of the MacBride Principles in New York. The Administration cannot allow its *special relationship* [emphasis added] with the British Government to bias its responses to issues dealing with Northern Ireland (4 August 1992)

One must question the role of the FBI in the proceedings against Francis Gildernew. At one point, an INS official explained to Francis Gildernew that the FBI had pressed for an arrest but that the INS had no interest in the case. After Gildernew's arrest, and without warning, the New York State Liquor Bureau posted a notice on the door of the pub, informing the public that the bar had closed. The notice included information that described Francis' political involvement in Ireland. Francis was not permitted to enter his place of business. The Gildernews and their supporters believe that the FBI had requested that the Liquor Bureau revoke the licencse. Eventually, the pub was re-opened under the direction of Sharon Gildernew, Francis' spouse.[9]

In late 1992 Gildernew was informed that a judicial decision would be reached by the following autumn. Within a few months, however, the INS requested that Gildernew visit its New York office and, strangely, officials there returned his confiscated passport and stamped his green card. Deportation proceedings were effectively dropped but without explanation.

So how did Gildernew win the fight? He attributes the win to the actions of his supporters. His arrest sparked the formation of a defence fund on his behalf. The group met weekly and organised several events for the purpose of drawing attention to Gildernew's plight. Countless fundraisers were held in small New York towns, such as East Durham, Tappan, Mohegan Lake and in larger cities, such as Yonkers and Westchester. Money was raised to pay bail, attorney fees and other expenses that occurred during the deportation proceedings. Tim Cotton, one of the main leaders of the defence committee, noted that many donations were small, but no less important. At times, he noted, people donated funds that would otherwise have been used to pay a household electric bill. Buses full of supporters travelled to deportation hearings in New York City, leaving Poughkeepsie in the early morning. Courtrooms were full of supporters, forcing many people to wait outside. Some supporters requested vacation leave from work to attend. Speeches were delivered in several towns and cities in New York, Pennsylvania and elsewhere. At one point Gildernew was asked to speak at the unveiling of a statue at Ellis Island, the famous US port of entry for thousands of immigrants. The symbolism was clearly important here. An extensive letter-writing campaign was established during which local, state and national political representatives were notified about Gildernew's case. This effort resulted in considerable support extended by these persons. The local Irish Northern Aid, non-existent in Poughkeepsie until the INS moved to deport Francis Gildernew, sought to maintain good relationships with several of his supporters. Congressman Ted Weiss died during the period of deportation proceedings. He had been an outspoken supporter of Francis' case. The defence group sent flowers to Weiss' family as a note of respect for the Congressman. And after deportation proceedings against Francis had been dropped by the INS, his defence group sponsored a dinner event to thank those politicians who were most supportive.[10] Persons so honoured were provided with 'Voice of Justice' awards. Francis Gildernew hopes for appropriate legislation that will prevent this from happening to other people: 'I don't care if they are from Ireland or Guatemala.'

Liam Ryan, a naturalised US citizen, returned to his native Ireland and was murdered with Michael Devlin by the Ulster

Volunteer Force (UVF) in 1989 (Cusack and McDonald 1997; Murray 1998, p. 182). A few years earlier Ryan had been convicted in the United States for the purchase of weapons by fraud (Wilson 1995). His status of naturalised US citizen prevented him from being deported from the United States. Regardless, he had returned to Ireland by choice and was subsequently assassinated by loyalist paramilitaries. No arrests have ever been made. Liam Ryan was a cousin of Francis Gildernew and Gildernew had resided with him upon first arriving in the United States. The murder of Liam Ryan raises the issue of whether the United States would bear responsibility for the safety of Francis Gildernew had he been deported.

At the time of Francis' arrest in 1992, the INS began to initiate deportation proceedings against several other Irish former political offenders residing in the United States. Known among supporters as the 'deportees', these persons included Charlie Caulfield, Kevin Crossan, Noel Gaynor, Gabriel Megahey, Robbie McErlean, Matt Morrison and Brian Pearson, among others. Their backgrounds were similar. Many had been involved in the civil rights movement in the north of Ireland. All had been arrested for what they believed to be political offences. Several had been subjected to internment whereby they were detained without charge for several months at a time. Most had been convicted in a Diplock court or juries comprised solely of all Protestants. Several of the deportees and their families utilised a collective approach to resist deportation and to highlight their cases to potential supporters, politicians and media. In this effort the families organised fundraisers, encouraged extensive letter-writing campaigns and applied pressure to US government officials.

Matt Morrison

Matt Morrison was under order of deportation for several years. His partner, Francie Broderick, is a woman of both substance and determination, and together she and Matt worked diligently to resist deportation. Matt Morrison gives great credit to Francie Broderick, to whom he refers as 'The Organiser': 'We are a good team', he acknowledged, 'her strengths are my weaknesses'.

Francie Broderick is a United States citizen and the couple have two children, both born in the United States. Fighting deportation became the focus of their daily lives. There were letters to be sent, rallies, speeches and fundraisers to be organised and attended, action plans to be developed and distributed to supporters. At one point Francie and Matt lobbied for support at the Democratic National Convention in Chicago. At another, Francie travelled to Ireland, her trip purposely coinciding with a visit to Ireland by President Clinton, in the hope of highlighting her husband's case. In a letter to supporters she wrote, 'Mostly I am going to Ireland because I am tired, my children are tired, we are worn down and tired of this fight.' The fight was exhausting and the family longed for normality (McClellan 1994).

During our discussion Matt Morrison spoke softly yet forcefully. He is a reluctant speaker (McClellan 1997) yet during still another speech to an American audience he patiently explained once again the situation in the north of Ireland and his experiences with deportation proceedings in the United States.

Morrison was 13 years old when British troops entered the north in 1969. He witnessed the events of 'Bloody Sunday' at the impressionable age of 16. He is a former member (self-admitted) of the IRA who spent ten years in Long Kesh for the attempted murder of an RUC officer and for possession of a weapon with intent. He fired the weapon, an act that he does not deny, although the officer was not hit.

He entered the United States in 1985 under his true identity, but responded 'no' when asked if he had ever been imprisoned for a crime in a foreign country. Shortly after arriving in the United States he married Francie, whom he had met and corresponded with during his imprisonment. The couple resided in St Louis, Missouri. After Morrison's arrival the family lived quietly but under mounting stress, wondering whether the INS would uncover his past. Eventually Matt contacted the INS, informed them of his status and requested political asylum. By INS standards

Matt's actions were indicative of 'good faith' (Schoultz 1992) yet deportation proceedings commenced shortly thereafter.

Matt requested a suspension of deportation on the basis that deportation would result in extreme hardship to him and to his family members (his spouse and his children were born in the United States). Indeed, suspension of deportation has been provided to others for this very reason. Had the request been approved, it would have in effect adjusted his status from that of a deportable alien to a permanent resident. The request, however, was denied in 1993; Matt appealed the decision but lost. In 1994, he applied for political asylum, but in 1995 this request was also denied. Persons may not be eligible for witholding deportation if the INS perceives that the individual had been involved in the persecution of others based on race, religion, nationality or other related factors. This reasoning was used in the decision to deny political asylum for Morrison.

Related Cases

Noel Gaynor was arrested in the north of Ireland in 1976 and served 14 years in prison. He emigrated to the United States in 1990 where he later married. In 1993 he was arrested and one year later he was found to be an 'excludable alien' because of his past conviction in the north of Ireland. As a result he had no legal right to seek political asylum. He was denied permanent residency because he had falsified his visa application. He was denied political asylum because of his past conviction in the north of Ireland.

In 1981 Gabe Megahey was convicted in the United States on a weaponry violation for attempting to purchase weapons for the IRA, one of the few deportees who had been convicted for violating US criminal law. He was sentenced to prison. The INS initiated deportation proceedings upon his release from prison. His request for political asylum was denied on the basis that he was alleged to have been involved in the 'persecution of others'.

The outcome of the case against Brian Pearson was quite different.[11] Pearson had served a 12-year prison sentence in

Long Kesh for participating in the bombing of a British army barracks. Upon his release he entered the United States in 1988 and married Doris Collins, a US citizen. In 1992 he applied for adjustment of status but three years later his request was denied. At one deportation hearing several assistant US attorneys were present, filling the front row (Boyer 1996a). He applied for political asylum and, after a lengthy deportation process, was granted asylum in March 1997. It was a major decision. Judge Phillip Williams ruled that:

> Government property, as opposed to 'the indiscriminate bombing of a civilian populace' was the target of said attack. Accordingly, the respondent's offences relating to that event will be deemed 'political' for this court's purposes (*Irish News* 1997a).

The judge ruled that the barracks represented a 'legitimate target...under international law and the laws of war' (Associated Press 1997a) and found that Pearson had demonstrated a fear of persecution if he were to be deported to Northern Ireland. The judge also noted that he considered RUC actions against Catholics as 'atrocious' (Associated Press 1997a). The US government had 30 days to appeal the asylum decision and did so, an action predicted by Francie Broderick, the wife of deportee Matt Morrison (*Irish News* 1997a).

Support

The financial and emotional costs are considerable for individuals who choose to fight deportation, costs which Schrecker (1996–1997, p. 416) referred to as the '...equally punitive byproducts of the [deportation] process'. Hearings and other proceedings are numerous, often lasting several years, and produce considerable financial strain and emotional exhaustion for the deportee and his or her family. The process encompasses the family whereby the primary focus is concentrated on fighting deportation. In some cases household income is strained as resources are earmarked for expenses relating to the deportation. Several persons facing deportation have not been permitted to earn wages, so that a spouse must often bear the primary responsibility for the family income. Persons requesting political asylum are not provided with free legal aid nor are they required to be represented by attorneys, although research shows that asylum approval rates are much higher for persons with legal representation. In some cases attorneys work pro bono but more often than not the individual is responsible for providing at least partial payment to cover attorneys' fees. There are other costs as well. Miscellaneous items such as telephone calls, faxes, photocopies and travel involve considerable expense. When several deportees and their families spoke at the special hearings of the Ad Hoc Congressional Committee on Irish Affairs in Washington, D.C. in 1997, one writer noted, 'There will be suits and dresses to have dry-cleaned, fares to and from Washington, taxi rides, meals, hotel bills and more baby sitters. All to get three hours in front of an ad hoc committee' (Mac an Bhaird 1997a).

Defence groups that have emerged on behalf of a number of the deportees have provided some financial assistance. These groups have organised various fundraisers and have encouraged a collective approach through writing letters to congressional members, staff with the US Justice Department and other officials. Adverts and notices are placed in US newspapers that cater primarily for Irish and Irish American readers. Defence funds have been established which assist the families. Many supporters contribute only a few dollars (although at times they might donate funds on more than one occasion). Matt Morrison noted that $1,000 was the largest sum of money donated to his defence from any one person (Farrow 1997). Defence funds, however, are quite limited in relation to the costs. Although donations to the Matt Morrison fund totalled more than $70,000, the financial costs of resisting deportation over the course of several years have greatly exceeded this figure. The emotional costs of resisting deportation are vast, albeit difficult to measure.

Deportation and the IRA Ceasefire

In the 14 months that followed the Easter Rising of 1916, the British government granted amnesty to Irish political prisoners. During the 1994–96 IRA ceasefire, the United States government had an opportunity to use deportation cases in a positive manner to promote the peace process. Proceedings against Irish republicans could have been dropped during this time. However, the United States government did not offer any concessions in these cases despite the lengthy IRA ceasefire that commenced in 1994. Amnesty was not forthcoming. In fact, during the ceasefire Charlie Caulfield was arrested and Matt Morrison was denied political asylum, as was Gabriel Megahey. Brian Pearson was denied adjustment of status, he appealed, was denied again, and handcuffed and detained briefly just after the February 1996 IRA bombing. During an ad hoc committee hearing of the US House of Representatives in February 1997, Congressman Peter King reported that a US diplomat in Dublin claimed that Scotland Yard '…was pressuring the United States to deport Irish nationalists' (Prebensen 1997). The British government strongly denied this claim, arguing instead that decisions relating to the deportations rested with US authorities (McCartan and Purdy 1997).

In September 1997, two months after a second IRA ceasefire was announced, the US Attorney-General, Janet Reno, dropped deportation proceedings against six deportees: Noel Gaynor, Gerald McDade, Robbie McErlean, Gabriel Megahey, Matt Morrison and Brian Pearson. Other cases, for example those involving Kevin Crossan and Charles Caulfield, were also affected. The decision was said to follow a recommendation from US Secretary of State Madeleine Albright. The Justice Department issued a statement that the decision did not reflect US approval of previous 'terrorist' activity and carefully noted that its decision had not been influenced by claims and reports (for example, fleeing political persecution) from the deportees. Nevertheless, the decision sent a powerful message that the US government recognised the political nature of the offences even if it did not acknowledge this officially. Evidence of this recognition was clear from the official statement issued by the US government in which it declared that the move was intended to further the *political* peace process (McAleer 1997a) [emphasis added]. And, interestingly, the deportation proceedings were suspended within a day of Sinn Féin signing on to the Mitchell Principles. Unionists in the north were infuriated by the US decision, believing the action to be influenced by a tri-government conspiracy (McCartan and Purdy 1997). The suspension of deportations in these cases in effect negated the British criminalisation policy aimed at IRA members in the north of Ireland.

The decision to suspend deportations for selected individuals received considerable publicity and in many ways represented a significant measure in the lives of several individuals who had fought deportation for several years. However, the implications of the suspensions have not been clear. At the time of this writing, nearly two years have passed since the deportation proceedings were suspended, yet to date none of the individuals has been issued an adjustment of status. In fact, deportation proceedings could re-commence at any time and such a decision could be influenced strongly by the termination of the current IRA ceasefire. Closure is lacking for the individuals to whom the suspensions applied, and for their families, yet the official line is that the suspensions are 'on hold,' and tied directly to the 'peace process' across the Atlantic. In effect, the 'deportees' still are.

Moreover, deportation proceedings are continuing against other Irish persons, such as Noel Cassidy in Cleveland, Ohio and John McNicholl in Philadelphia, Pennsylvania. Cassidy was convicted in 1979 in a Diplock court, served time in Long Kesh and arrived in the United States after his release from prison. He was arrested in 1990 and charged with illegal entry into the United States. He married a US citizen but was subsequently divorced. A current resident of Cleveland, he teaches Irish language courses at a local college. In light of the divorce, Cassidy was denied adjustment of status in April 1999.

John Eddie McNicholl escaped from Long Kesh in 1976 with nine other republican prisoners. He lived in County

Donegal until 1984, at which time he and his wife moved to the United States. His spouse was granted US citizenship and all of their children were born in the United States.

McNicholl had resided in the United States for eleven years before deportation proceedings commenced in Philadelphia in 1995. Several RUC officers travelled to the United States, at US government expense, to provide testimony against McNicholl. At the time of writing, proceedings are continuing.

The Justice Department did not suspend deportation proceedings against John McNicholl, as it did for several other Irish former political prisoners. A participant writer to an Internet discussion on Irish politics raised the issue as to whether deportation proceedings against McNicholl have continued largely because of his prior affiliation with the Irish National Liberation Army (INLA) rather than the IRA. Regardless of ideological and other differences among republican groups, this suggestion is an important one; although the INLA has been on ceasefire since August 1998, its members remain opposed to the Good Friday Agreement.

Summary

During a 1995 interview, Matt Morrison stated that he missed Ireland – it's people, their wit, the sea. I asked him under what conditions he would return to Ireland freely. He stated, 'I'd return if my family had no fear of discrimination or of assassination. [The possibility] of assassination is the real issue.' And so it is. In spite of a loyalist ceasefire that was announced in October 1994, several Catholics have been murdered by loyalists since that time (see Chapter 5). News reports from Northern Ireland and from the United States have continued to use the terms 'loyalist ceasefire' or at best, the 'crumbling loyalist ceasefire' as if it were still intact. The issue is not whether the ceasefire was still in place but whether it had ever been in place. Often referred to as 'Catholic civilians', the majority of the victims of loyalist violence had not been involved with any paramilitary group prior to their deaths. Matt Morrison is a former member of the IRA, a history to which he admits. The other deportees all served prison sentences in Northern Ireland for political offences. Several have acknowledged past membership in Sinn Féin. If deported, would they not be more likely than 'uninvolved Catholic civilians' to be targeted by loyalists? Who would defend them and their respective families from loyalist attack in the north of Ireland? If deported, it is distinctly possible that they would be more likely to be targeted by loyalists than politically uninvolved Catholics. Deportations would be risky ventures in this regard.

To date, the British government has released dozens of paramilitary prisoners as part of the Good Friday Agreement and this policy reflects a spirit of amnesty. Although the US government suspended deportations for several individuals in 1997, no official action has been forthcoming since that time. It is of great concern that individual lives can be affected in such a manner by a political process over which they have little or no influence. Further, it is naïve to assume that the IRA perceives the suspensions as a 'carrot,' that is, an incentive to maintain their ceasefire.

Deportation proceedings involving Irish republicans in the United States are affected by foreign policy considerations, namely the US–Britain alliance. However, the legislative history of the US 1980 Refugee Act did not intend political factors, including foreign relations, to influence asylum and other immigration decisions. In light of that history, the executive branch has developed its own rules.

3

Extradition

> '...and finally when I drowned the cell lights and darkened the room enough to observe from my westward window those little points of light (the stars); Rigel, Aldebaron, Procyon, Capella, Caster & Pollock, and the dog Star, Serius, the brightest star in the heavens, I can for a while leave here and think of deeper things, though I oftimes wonder if there are any jails up there.' *Pól Brennan, 'Starry, Starry Nights' Anderson Valley Advertiser, 2 February 1994a*

In the 1940s, Menachem Begin participated in and advocated violence in hopes of a British withdrawal from Palestine. At one point the British government offered an award of £10,000 for Begin's capture. Kelly (1992) questioned whether the United States would have agreed to a British extradition request had Begin sought refuge in the United States (in later years, as Kelly notes, Begin was awarded the Nobel Peace Prize).

For nearly a century the United States recognised a political offence exception to extradition so that persons accused or convicted elsewhere of politically-motivated offences were exempt from extradition. In the nineteenth century and for most of the twentieth century, this defence to extradition had been included in nearly all extradition treaties involving the United States and other countries (Farrell 1985). Extradition history changed dramatically in 1986, with the passage of the US–UK Supplementary Treaty, a document that was influenced greatly by the special relationship between the United States and Britain.

Extradition Warrants: 1977 to 1986

Between 1977 and 1986, extradition decisions between the United States and Britain were based on the guidelines outlined in 28 U.S.T. 228, the 1977 extradition treaty between the two countries. Only a few Irish republicans were targeted for extradition during those years and among those persons for whom extradition warrants were issued, judges typically found the offences to be politically motivated, thus extradition to Britain was denied. These cases are highlighted below.

Desmond Mackin

In 1978, Desmond Mackin was charged in Northern Ireland with the attempted murder of a British soldier. He later entered the United States where he was arrested in 1980. The US government issued an extradition warrant after Britain requested Mackin's return. Extradition proceedings commenced thereafter, at which point Mackin denied the charges. The magistrate ruled that the evidence of attempted murder was insufficient, but that the case would be reviewed on the charge of possessing and firing a weapon.

The court found that Mackin's offences were political and therefore he could not be extradited. The magistrate used three criteria in determining the political nature of the offence and denying extradition: 1) that a political uprising was occurring at the time when, and place where, Mackin committed the offence; 2) that Mackin was a member of an uprising group, that is, the IRA in this case; and 3) that Mackin's offence was related to the political uprising and 'in furtherance of' its goals. An appellate court affirmed the decision in 1981.

US law allows the INS to initiate deportation proceedings even when extradition has been denied for political offences. Stated differently, a person can 'win' or succeed in an extradition hearing, but be deported from the United States by the INS for entering the United States illegally. Moreover, immigration officials are *not* required to consider the evidence and outcome of an extradition hearing. Or, where political offences are involved individuals must demonstrate the political nature of the case in an extradition hearing and if extradition is denied, an immigration hearing is likely to follow during which persons must show a well-founded fear of persecution if s/he were returned to the home country.

In Mackin's case, the INS initiated deportation hearings after the extradition warrant failed.[1] Persons facing deportation can choose a country to which they wish to be deported if that country will accept them. Mackin chose to be deported to the south of Ireland rather than risk deportation to British authorities.[2] The British government never issued an extradition warrant to the south of Ireland for Mackin's return. This decision may have been based on the belief that the judiciary in the south would also have found Mackin to be non-extraditable or perhaps because the US judiciary failed to find probable cause to support a charge of attempted murder. Alternatively, a successful extradition from the south of Ireland would have embarrassed the US government in that the move would appear even more like a 'disguised extradition' from the United States. Asylum and extradition often have contradictory goals (Bassiouni 1996) and an extradition request issued to a second government to which the US deported the accused would have highlighted this contradiction.

Peter McMullen

Peter McMullen, one-time member of a parachute regiment of the British army, deserted in the 1970s, joined the IRA, and in 1974 participated in bomb attacks against military posts in Yorkshire, England. He later entered the United States, surrendered in San Francisco in 1978 and requested political asylum claiming that he would be targeted by the IRA after informing on some of its members. The British government issued an extradition warrant, the first since 1903 for an Irish political offender (Farrell 1985). Paul O'Dwyer's[3] firm assisted the defence; McMullen was not popular in Irish American republican circles but O'Dwyer and his colleagues focused on the larger picture (that is, the legal precedent regarding the extradition of Irish Republicans, former or otherwise) rather than on McMullen's reputation as an informant (Wilson 1995).

The extradition warrant was dismissed by a US judge in 1979, who used two criteria in denying extradition: 1) that McMullen's offence occurred during the time of a political uprising; and 2) that McMullen was a member of the uprising group. Although McMullen was not extradited to Britain at this time, deportation proceedings commenced shortly thereafter. Eventually, McMullen requested to be deported to the south of Ireland. On the day of the scheduled deportation, and just after the Supplementary Treaty (discussed below) became effective, the US government approved a second extradition request from Britain (Bassiouni 1996). Proceedings against McMullen commenced again and the extradition request was granted. McMullen was extradited to Britain after spending nine years incarcerated in the United States awaiting either deportation or extradition hearings. His case, however, generated little support from Irish America (O'Hanlon 1996), largely because of his status as an IRA informant.

William (Liam) Quinn

William (Liam) Quinn is a US citizen by birth. Although born and raised in the United States he allegedly became an IRA volunteer. He was subsequently convicted and imprisoned in the south of Ireland for IRA membership, returning to the United States in 1978 shortly after his release (Farrell 1985). Quinn was arrested in California by FBI agents in 1981 after the US government approved an extradition request from British authorities.

The British government alleged that Quinn had participated in the murder of a London police officer in 1975.[4] The extradition warrant was issued several years after the killing and reports indicated that the British knew of Quinn's whereabouts and could have arrested him eleven weeks after the offence had occurred. The passing of a number of years made it difficult for Quinn to locate witnesses and to recall his alibi (Clarizio 1988).

In 1982 a magistrate used the same criteria outlined in the Mackin case but refused to apply the political offence exception because the act had occurred in England, rather than in Northern Ireland. Moreover, the magistrate concluded that Quinn had not provided enough evidence to verify his membership of the IRA. A reversal came one year later when a judge ruled that the magistrate had erred and concluded that Quinn's actions were political in nature. Extradition was therefore denied. The US government appealed, in which case the Ninth Circuit Court affirmed the first ruling, holding that the political 'uprising' did not extend to England. Accordingly, had Quinn's actions occurred in Northern Ireland, the political offence exception would have applied and extradition would have been denied.[5] Quinn was extradited to Britain where in 1988 he was convicted of murder and received a life sentence. He was imprisoned in England but requested a transfer to the south of Ireland. He was released from Portlaoise prison in April 1999.

The legal reasoning in the Quinn case was contradictory. The appellate court ruled that the uprising did not extend to England, but in their decision the court referred to Quinn's conviction in the south of Ireland where he was tried 'in a special court utilized for the trial of political cases' (Ninth Circuit 1986, p. 783). They referred to his imprisonment in the south of Ireland for which Quinn was 'categorized in Dublin as a "special category prisoner" – a political prisoner incarcerated in a manner akin to prisoner-of-war status' (Ninth Circuit 1986, p. 783). The court then appeared to acknowledge Quinn's political status during his incarceration in the south of Ireland. From this acknowledgement the court indirectly suggested that the uprising extended to the south of Ireland. Its refusal to recognise that the uprising extended to England was illogical.

In the McMullen case, the British sought extradition for an alleged offence committed in England, yet extradition was denied because McMullen's actions were determined to be political in nature. Quinn's actions were also alleged to have occurred in England, yet the court found that the site of the offence was external to the uprising in the north of Ireland, 'An uprising is both temporally and spatially limited' (Ninth Circuit 1986, p. 817).

Quinn's US citizenship would have been advantageous had he succeeded in fighting extradition, for that status would have prevented his deportation. However, citizenship may also have contributed to his extradition in that judges may have found it difficult to apply the political offence exception to an American who left the United States in order to take part in a political uprising elsewhere. In fact, the Ninth Circuit Court stated that it did not consider '...whether Quinn's status as a citizen of an uninvolved nation would also preclude him from receiving the protection of the [political offence] exception' (1986, p. 818). However, the dissenting judge[6] in the case stated: 'I do not believe that mercenaries or volunteers in a foreign conflict can claim protection under the political offense exception. I deduce from Judge Reinhardt's views on international terrorism that he would agree' (Ninth Circuit 1986, p. 820).

James Barr

James Barr was arrested in Philadelphia in 1984 after the British government had issued an extradition warrant. Extradition, however, was denied in 1986.[7] The judicial decision was based not on the political nature of the offence; rather, the judge noted that evidence which linked Barr to the alleged offence was lacking (Wilson 1995). On two separate occasions Barr had been arrested in the north of Ireland based on the testimony of paid informers who implicated republican paramilitaries. One informer later retracted his statements. The second informer was Harry Kirkpatrick, whose uncorroborated testimony resulted in the convictions of 25 persons. Eventually all 25 had their convictions overturned (Greer 1990). The US ruling that found a lack of probable cause reflects the differences between minimum legal standards of US and British law as applied to political offenders. The details provided in the extradition warrant by the British governement failed to meet the minimum legal standards under US law (that is, 'probable cause'). Barr still faced deportation proceedings and was held in US custody for 17 months without charge. He was finally granted political asylum in 1993, although the US government appealed that decision.

Amendments to the Political Offence Exception

The United States sought to 'narrow' the political offence exception primarily in its treaties with its 'close allies' (Nadelmann 1993, p. 828). The extradition treaty with Britain was no exception; in fact, modifications to the US–UK extradition treaty in 1986 reflected the most substantial change ever to US extradition law. The US treaty with Britain was the first of its kind to be altered. Collectively, the changes were referred to as the US–UK Supplementary Extradition Treaty, passed by the United States Congress, approved by the British Parliament, and effective from 23 December 1986.

The Supplementary Treaty was passed in the decade during which the special relationship between the United States and Britain was at its strongest ever. The alliance between President Ronald Reagan and Prime Minister Margaret Thatcher resulted in a significant change in United States extradition policy, thereby ending a long history of providing refuge for Irish political offenders.

The introduction of the Supplementary Treaty by President Reagan was a *direct* reflection of the relationship between the United States and British governments at the time. Three court rulings found IRA members[8] to be nonextraditable because courts had employed the political offence exception and refused to extradite. Rulings from these extradition hearings incited the British government and also offended the United States Justice and State Departments (Banoff and Pyle 1984). Thatcher desperately wanted IRA suspects in the United States to be extradited to Britain. Ogden (1990) noted that Thatcher's interest in the extradition cases was one contributory factor in her decision to support the Anglo-Irish Agreement.[9] Thatcher believed that if she did not endorse the Agreement, the United States would be less likely to assist with the extradition process.

Opponents of the political offence exception warned that the United States would become a 'safe haven for terrorists' (Riley 1986, p. 3). History showed differently; by 1985 the political offence exception had been applied 76 times in 140 years and successfully used as a defence to extradition on only four occasions (Bassiouni 1985). In fact, the British government had issued a minimum of 64 extradition warrants in a 20-year period to US officials and all but three had been extradited. In each of the three cases for which extradition had failed, the persons accused were alleged to be IRA members (Kelly 1992), former or otherwise.

Writers and legal scholars have traced the Supplementary Treaty passage to the 1986 US attack on Libya (Cronin 1987; Dillon 1992; Kelly 1992). After the Treaty was introduced by Ronald Reagan in 1985, the Senate vote was postponed for nearly a year during which time Margaret Thatcher permitted the United States to launch planes from airbases in Britain. In fact, Britain was the only European country to provide support for the United States in its attacks on Libya (Dobson 1995). President Reagan then announced publicly that allowing (IRA) 'terrorists' to remain in the United States would be offensive to Thatcher (Riley 1986, p. 3).[10] A *London Times* (1986) editorial asked: 'Is it not time for the government of the United States to pay a debt?' And, relating the Treaty debates with the US attack on Libya, an act which the British government supported, the editorial told United States senators: 'you owe us one'.

The US debt was paid. The Treaty eliminated the century-old political offence exception while including the less forceful Article 3(a) which permits a defence to extradition if, by preponderance of the evidence, the accused demonstrates that the extradition request itself is politically motivated or demonstrates that s/he *will be* prejudiced at trial or punished on account of race, religion, nationality or political opinion. Moreover, the Treaty was retroactive and specified that nearly all violent offences were extraditable, regardless of the political nature of the case. In effect, the offences outlined for extradition in the new Treaty coincided neatly with the list of scheduled offences[11] in the north of Ireland (Iversen 1989).

Joseph Doherty

Foreign relations between the United States and Britain clearly affected the extradition proceedings and the subsequent deportation of Joseph Doherty; this issue has been discussed at great length by writers and legal scholars (Dillon 1992; Kelly 1992; Roebuck 1994). In December 1984, prior to the passage of the Supplementary Treaty, a federal judge in New York concluded that Doherty's offences were political in nature and ruled against extradition. The judge based the decision on five factors: 1) the nature of its offence; 2) the context of the offence; 3) the status of the accused, that is, whether the offence was committed for the defendant's own purposes or for the goals of the organisation involved in the political uprising; 4) the nature of the organisation; and 5) whether the act occurred within the physical environment of the political uprising. The US government appealed the judge's ruling, yet in 1985 an appellate court affirmed the district court's decision and as a result Doherty was successful in his fight against official extradition.

Doherty had requested political asylum but withdrew the request in September 1986. Anticipating that the Supplementary Treaty would be passed and a second extradition warrant would be issued (Dillon 1992), Doherty therefore requested to be deported to the south of Ireland (immigration policy provides that persons facing deportation may request to be deported to a country of their choice, rather than to the country of origin). The INS challenged Doherty's request but in 1987 the Board of Immigration Appeals rejected the government's argument, providing the go-ahead for deportation to the south of Ireland. The United States Attorney-General, however, has discretion in these matters and two Attorney-Generals mentioned foreign relations with Britain as reasons for denying Doherty's request. For the first time ever, the Justice Department considered United States foreign policy in its decision to reject a person's request to be deported to a country of his or her choice (Kelly 1992). In February 1992, Joseph Doherty was returned to British authorities in the north of Ireland.[12]

Doherty had received considerable support from America. At one stage, an amicus brief was submitted to the US Supreme Court on his behalf, signed by 132 members of Congress (O'Hanlon 1998b). He lost as a result of a combined effort by the United States and British governments. In effect, Doherty's case demonstrated that the executive branch would go to great lengths, including the violation of the separation of powers clause of the US constitution (Hughes 1997a), in order to exclude persons from the US, all for the sake of foreign relations.

The legal pursuit of Joe Doherty disturbed supporters, politicians and writers. Discrepancies were noted based on an individual's country of origin. For example, in 1985 and in 1987 the United States permitted hundreds of political prisoners and their families from Cuba to enter the United States (Domínguez 1992; Hamm 1991). Cockburn (1990) described the case of Orlando Bosch, who was involved in the bombing of a Japanese freighter off the coast of Florida as well as the bombings of eight tourist offices in the United States which had allegedly conducted trade with Cuba. Bosch was eventually convicted in the United States for a gun attack on a foreign freighter in Miami. Later released, he was re-arrested for violating parole. His plea for political asylum was rejected. Strong pressure from Cuban groups in Miami, however, contributed to his being paroled and freed in the United States. Cockburn compared the case to that of Joe Doherty and suggested that: 'The Irishman should hispanicize his name, make more influential friends in Miami and start threatening Fidel Castro.'

Nadelmann (1993) suggested that, historically, the United States has used deportation (rather than extradition) as a tool to return fugitives to their county of origin. Shearer (1971) suggested that 'de facto extradition' might occur more frequently than official extradition; the former refers to those cases in which persons are deported (rather than extradited) to the very country that seeks to try or punish them. Doherty was deported and not extradited, despite reports to the contrary. Kelly (1992) observed that a *New York Times* headline incorrectly stated that Doherty had been extradited but retracted the headline thereafter. Other news reports also incorrectly stated that he had been extradited (see for instance, Irish American Information Service 1998; McCoy 1998). Even Martin Dillon got it wrong when he noted that Doherty had been extradited (1992, p. 248). History has suggested that deportation has been used to target persons in the absence of '...other mechanisms of repression...' (Schrecker 1996–1997, p. 401). And so it was for Joseph Doherty.

The H-Block 4

In the early 1990s extradition proceedings commenced in California against four men from Northern Ireland: Kevin Barry Artt, Pól Brennan, Terence Kirby and Jimmy Smyth. Known collectively as the H-Block 4,[13] each took part in what has been described as largest mass escape from prison in British history, in September 1983.

After residing in the United States for several years, Jimmy Smyth was arrested in 1992 and extradition proceedings commenced thereafter. Like Doherty, Smyth succeeded at the initial extradition hearing after a United States District Judge found that the evidence satisfied an exemption or defence to extradition. The US government appealed the judge's ruling during the IRA ceasefire and, in July 1995, the Ninth Circuit Court of Appeals reversed the District Court's decision. The appellate court based its ruling on Article 3(a) of the extradition treaty which requires individuals to show fear of persecution. Smyth's attorneys showed evidence of *past* persecution, and the court acknowledged such, but ruled that the defence had failed to demonstrate that Smyth would be persecuted in the *future*. The decision left several interested parties and political analysts wondering how 'future persecution' could be demonstrated. Shortly thereafter Smyth's attorney, Karen Snell, stated in a letter to Gerry Adams: '...the Ninth Circuit's opinion was influenced by a *faulty understanding of the peace process* [emphasis added] to date. They appear to believe that any danger republican ex-prisoners may have faced upon their release from prison has ceased' (cited in O'Neill 1995a).

Smyth appealed for a hearing en banc (that is, to be heard by all appellate judges in the Circuit after the ruling by the three-member panel). The Justice Department fought hard – even opposing an application by the Lawyers Alliance to file an amicus brief ('friend of the court')[14] on Smyth's behalf. Again, during the ceasefire, the Court of Appeals agreed with the prosecution and denied the application to file an amicus brief, and more important, denied a rehearing en banc in January 1996.

Foreign relations between Britain and the United States began to deteriorate during the period 1994 to 1996. The alliance was affected a great deal by President Clinton's faith in Gerry Adams, who during this time was granted visitor visas and permitted to raise funds in the United States (see Chapter 6). In fact some have suggested that the 'special relationship', established earlier in the twentieth century and cemented during the Reagan and Bush years, had soured substantially (O'Clery 1995).

Despite the friction between the two governments, Jimmy Smyth was bound over for extradition.[15] The United States Secretary of State Warren Christopher signed the extradition papers in August 1996, at which point Smyth was returned to the north of Ireland.[16] Within a few weeks, the United States launched its attack on Iraq and days later John Major publicly stated his support for the United States for its invasion of Iraq, citing Clinton's courage. Shortly thereafter, Secretary of State Warren Christopher extended his appreciation to John Major for his support of the United States' attack. The relationship between the United States and Britain was beginning to sound 'special' again. As others have noted, one of Clinton's campaign promises was that there would be 'no more Joe Dohertys' (Boyer 1996b). In light of the 1996 extradition of Jimmy Smyth, Clinton failed to keep that promise.

One cannot help but wonder whether the Smyth extradition prompted the British interest in pursuing the extradition of Dermot McNally from the south of Ireland. McNally also escaped from Long Kesh in 1983 and had lived in the south for years. Within two months of Smyth's return, press reports indicated that McNally had 'been traced to the

Irish Republic' (Marshall 1996) but McNally's residence was well known even in some Irish circles in the United States. In 1990 the Irish Supreme Court refused to grant the extradition of two other 1983 escapees. It is possible, therefore, that the British government believed that Smyth's extradition would exert pressure on the Irish judiciary to grant British extradition requests.

The cases of Jimmy Smyth and Joe Doherty serve as a striking contrast to the case of Peter McMullen, whose case was described earlier in this chapter. Doherty and Smyth were returned to the north of Ireland through defacto and official extradition, respectively. McMullen was extradited and returned to Britain in 1996 where he was subsequently convicted in York Crown Court for the offence of bombing a British military barracks. He was sentenced to 14 years. However, the judge took into account two factors: 1) evidence produced at McMullen's trial included previous public disclosure that he had renounced violence and the IRA; and 2) the time McMullen spent in US jails awaiting extradition hearings and fighting deportation. As a resut, McMullen was released after being credited with time served elsewhere.

Doherty spent nine years in US jails and Smyth was also incarcerated in the United States for several years, yet upon their return neither was credited with time served in the United States. Doherty admitted membership in the IRA; Smyth acknowledged affiliation with Sinn Féin. Neither, however, 'renounced violence' as did McMullen (Naughton 1996) and neither served as an informant for the British.

In January 1993, Pól Brennan was arrested in the United States on a passport violation after a fingerprint check linked him with the extradition warrant. He has been fighting extradition ever since. Initially incarcerated in the Oakland (California) City Jail, he was transferred in October 1995 to the federal detention centre where, for the first time in 19 months, he was permitted an open visit with his wife, Joanna.

At the time of our visit it had been 19 years since Pól had last set foot in the north of Ireland – a free person. By September 1995 he had been incarcerated in the United States for nearly two years, without formally being charged with any crime. His optimism was fading when he acknowledged, 'I don't know if or when I'll start to live any kind of normal existence'. At the age of 21 he was interned[17] in the north of Ireland for one year without charge. He was arrested two years later in 1976 and subsequently sentenced to 16 years for possessing explosives. In 1983, along with 37 other prisoners, he escaped from Long Kesh prison.

Pól was soft-spoken and relaxed during our visit. Concerned deeply about social and economic problems in the United States, he discussed 'the erosion of the industrial base', 'the increasing poverty level' and drug-related crime. At times his knowledge of crime and the US criminal justice system paralleled that of an academic criminologist. He noted, for example, 'the myth of a major crime wave' in the United States and voiced concern about the US prison system which he views as 'purely punitive' and likely 'to haunt this country down the line.'

He loves astronomy – and that knowledge helped guide the way during night travel after the escape. He wrote from his jail cell about topics such as the 1983 escape and the experiences shortly thereafter (Brennan 1994a), the 1994 IRA ceasefire (Brennan 1994b), and an Irish man's life in a US jail (Brennan 1993). I asked him his reasons for writing, to which he replied: 'I'd feel guilty if I didn't write.' He corresponds with other writers, such as Noam Chomsky and journalist Alexander Cockburn, both of whom have supported his quest for freedom.

In conversation, he recalled the sectarianism in the factory in which he worked as a young man. A Catholic co-worker had been murdered, Protestant co-workers boasted about the burning of Bombay Street and he had been threatened on numerous occasions.

A modest person in the truest sense, he describes feeling 'uncomfortable' when he, Artt, Kirby and Smyth were named grand marshals of the San Francisco St Patrick's Day parade, an honour in Irish American communities.

Detained without bail, Pól longed to be released. His family, a spouse and step-daughter, lived nearby and he craved normality. Unlike most defendants processed in the US criminal justice system, there is no presumption of bail in extradition hearings. Criteria used to deny bail include a judge or magistrate's determination of flight risk or the perception that the accused is a danger to the community. Yet Irish republicans nearly always comply with bail/bond requirements. During his lengthy incarceration in Long Kesh, Matt Morrison was able to recall only one fellow republican who failed to comply with bail regulations by not returning. Seamus Moley noted that, 'People can't be selfish. [Complying with bail/bond requirements] mirrors the Irish struggle – there should be no personal gain.' Kevin McKinley agreed, 'The struggle is not selfish – it is for the whole community.' Failure to comply with bail requirements would risk American support and its role in the overall republican struggle in the north of Ireland.

Although bail is not automatic, judges have the authority to consider special circumstances in granting bail. A few months after I visited Pól, he, Artt and Kirby were finally granted bail. By that time the three – still uncharged – had spent over two years in US jails. Artt and Brennan were each released on $500,000 bail; Kirby's bail was $1,000,000.

On 11 August 1997 a judge granted the extradition of all three men. The same judge had granted bail 20 months earlier, but revoked it at that time. The defence appealed both the bail revocation and the extradition decision. In February 1998, Mo Mowlam, Secretary of State for Northern Ireland, publicly stated her support for bail for the three Irishmen.

Within two months of their return to jail the three were separated. Pól was punished in solitary confinement after arguing that as a (remand) non-sentenced prisoner, he should not be forced to work in jail (Mac an Bhaird 1997b).

An appellate court affirmed the bail decision in October 1997 so that the three men remained incarcerated. One day after the US appellate ruling, Tony Kelly, another 1983 Long Kesh escapee, was released on bail in the south of Ireland. Bail was set at £40,000 – of which one-half was provided by a TD[18] from County Donegal, Ireland, where Kelly had lived openly for four years.[19]

In October 1998, an appellate court in California reversed the extradition orders by the district court which had ruled against Artt, Brennan and Kirby. The appellate decision directed the lower court to examine more closely whether the men had received unfair treatment during the British legal proceedings that led to their convictions in the north of Ireland. The appellate court determined that the lower court had not 'probed deeply enough into the possibility that the three men would be punished because of race, religion or political opinion'. In sum, the appellate court directed the district court to explore whether the legal system in the north of Ireland is fair and just.

In January 1998, this author received a letter from Pól Brennan in which he wrote, '...there has arisen a window of opportunity in my particular case that may allow me to revisit my motion before the district court to have my case heard under the old Treaty rather than the revised Supplementary Treaty. If I'm successful in getting the judge to look at this issue again...my claim will be heard under the political exception clause of the original treaty.' The 1986 Treaty specified that persons convicted of certain offences could not claim the political offence exception. Pól was convicted in the north of Ireland for the offences of possession of explosives and unlawful possession of a weapon. The 1986 Treaty specifies that 'an offense involving the use of a bomb, grenade, firearm, letter or parcel bomb, or any incendiary device' shall not be considered to be a political offence, and therefore extradition would apply in these cases. In other words, the 1986 Treaty mentions the 'use' of firearms or explosives, and Brennan argued that possession of these items is not equivalent to 'use', even where use is intended. He therefore asserted that his case should have been heard under the earlier 1977 Treaty with Britain rather than the more stringent 1986 Treaty. Brennan's window of opportunity opened a bit when, nine months later, the appellate court held that his case should indeed have been decided under the 1977 Treaty. The appellate decision returns the case to the district court which will make its determination under the earlier treaty, a treaty which uses a more broadly defined political offence exception to extradition.[20]

The decision over whether to continue to fight extradition is crucial and at times difficult. For Pól, the extradition will result in his return to Long Kesh where he will serve three years. If, however, the British policy of half-remission applies, Pól would serve between 18 and 20 months. If the British government were to credit him with time served in the United States, he would be a 'free' man. Alternatively, if he were to return and give up the fight against extradition, he could complete the sentence in Long Kesh and avoid an extended period of incarceration in the United States.

So why fight extradition? Why spend years in US jails without being charged with a crime, without being sentenced, knowing that there is a good possibility that you may be returned anyway? Because there is a glimmer of hope, a small chance for a win. And for Pól Brennan a win would mean life in the United States with his US-born wife, Joanna, and his step-daughter, Molly. A win just might set precedent. A win would send a powerful message from the US judiciary: that there is reason to fear political persecution in the north of Ireland.

But even if Brennan, Artt, and Kirby succeed in fighting extradition, they could still face deportation for entering the United States illegally. Imagine: After spending years in US jails and emerging as free persons from a federal court only to be handcuffed by the INS on the courthouse steps. Such as system smacks of hypocrisy.

Evidence produced by the defence during the extradition hearings of Kevin Barry Artt and Terry Kirby included data collected in the 1990s that showed a pattern of anti-Catholic bigotry among RUC officers (Ellison 1997) and evidence from several other cases in which defendants in the north of Ireland succeeded at the appellate level because of findings of perjury by government informants. Other escapees, when recaptured, were subjected to beatings and severe verbal abuse by prison guards. For example, in the extradition hearing of James Smyth, the US District Court (863 F. Supp. 1137,1146) noted the following as a 'finding of fact':

> The republican prisoners who escaped but were captured and returned were forced to run a gauntlet of guard dogs, which were allowed to bite them. The guards ordered attack dogs upon the republican prisoners as they were

moved to other cell blocks. The dogs bit several prisoners. The prisoners were denied medical care for several days... Upon their return to the Maze, prison officers kicked and punched the returned escapees....

In fact, assaults on Irish republicans by guards in Northern Ireland are now acknowledged by the judiciary in Northern Ireland. For example, in 1998 Irish republican and former political prisoner, Martin Meehan, was awarded £14,000 for injuries he sustained during a beating by prison officers ten years earlier. The physical assault resulted in a one-week hospital stay. Compensation for injuries of £30,000 was awarded to David Adams in 1998 for being physically assaulted by police officers while in their custody (Doran 1998). Among other injuries, Adams had suffered a punctured lung and fractured leg and ribs. The Committee on the Administration of Justice (1998, p. 2) concluded that his injuries '...amounted to torture as defined in the Convention Against Torture'.

The extradition cases in California also included testimony from David Baxendale, an English forensic scientist, who reported that police notes allegedly taken during Artt's interrogation appeared to have been rewritten; the notes were provided by the British government for the extradition hearing. In 1996, representatives from the Irish American Unity Conference reported that two British officials produced a 56-page document to be used for preparing witnesses appearing against Artt and Kirby in the extradition hearing (O'Coileain 1996). Judge Legge refused to hear evidence regarding the murder of Pat Finucane, a Belfast solicitor and Catholic who was murdered in 1989, although several human rights organisations have called for an independent inquiry into Finucane's death, citing allegations of collusion between loyalist paramilitaries and police (Amnesty International 1995; Lawyers Committee for Human Rights 1996b). Extraditions are not permitted from the United States if the accused can demonstrate a 'fear or well-founded fear of persecution.' How can an accused demonstrate this fear? How else to show threats by loyalists or security forces without mentioning other cases in the past in which

Catholics have been murdered? On two occasions defence attorneys from the United States have requested the British to reveal the contents of the Stalker Report, an investigation that allegedly uncovered a shoot-to-kill policy by security forces in Northern Ireland. Twice the British have refused to submit the document, despite judicial orders to do so. Therefore, several potentially important pieces of defence evidence were not admissable, although it is unclear whether the excluded documents would have altered the judicial outcome.

Summary

Farrell (1985) described the change in legal response in the south of Ireland that occurred in the 1970s. In the early part of that decade, IRA volunteers from the north were rarely arrested by gardaí (police in the south of Ireland) who appeared to turn a blind eye to IRA activities in the south. Moreover, despite the fact that several extradition warrants were issued by the British, no extraditions occurred, suggesting that the judiciary in the south considered IRA offences in the north to be political. Farrell noted that the British began to exert pressure on the south in 1972, emphasising that extraditions were necessary if the government of the south was to have any influence on the north. Shortly thereafter extradition warrants from the north began to result in arrests of IRA members. 'Foreign' policy played an important role in affecting the change in south-to-north extradition procedure. In the early 1980s, government officials from the south of Ireland voiced criticisms of the legal system in the north yet in 1984 Dominic McGlinchey became the first Irish republican to be extradited from the south to the north since 1922 (Farrell 1985). The government in the south bowed to pressure from Unionist politicians in the north and from the British government. Successful bids to extradite from south to north provided further justification for the United States to extradite Irish republicans who sought refuge from within its own territory.

Foreign relations with Britain have affected the extradition process involving Irish republicans in the United States. A subtle connection can be found between extradition proceedings and the gratitude extended for reciprocal support provided during times of war and conflict. The extradition cases reviewed herein raise issues of concern whereby US law was not broken but bent in order to appease a foreign ally. One concern focuses on Peter McMullen's case, whereby the second extradition request came through at the same time that he was scheduled for deportation to the south of Ireland. Was deportation intentionally delayed by the INS for the purpose of forcing McMullen into the jurisdiction of the British? The timing was not coincidental. Britain needed McMullen. How better than to send a message to the IRA that former members who worked to discredit the organisation would be treated with leniency? Joseph Doherty also believed that the INS was dragging its feet in his case, with delays and appeals in their hopes that a second extradition warrant would be issued after the 1986 Treaty became effective. These cases highlight the fact that extradition and deportation are not separate tools for exclusion; rather, the latter is a substitute for the former when all else fails.

Quinn's case is also of concern. Had Quinn succeeded in fighting extradition, his US citizenship would have protected him from deportation. Of the four pre-1986 cases that involved Irish republicans (former or otherwise), three were deported (Doherty, Mackin and McMullen) but Quinn, the only US citizen of the four, was extradited; perhaps because there was no other outlet available to return him to Britain.

The cases involving Mackin and Barr are a third concern. US judges in these cases ruled that the evidence was insufficient to support the extradition warrant. It is possible that the US government endorsed the extradition warrants because it believed that approval for the warrants was sufficient demonstration of support for its ally.

4

Prosecution

'...beyond these shores, wherever two or more Irishmen are gathered together, much can be done'. *Thomas Francis Meagher, writing from Richmond Prison (cited in O'Cathaoir 1990, p. 117)*

'It is our view that the Provisional IRA no longer have the resources or the support within the community to mount a prolonged campaign.' *J. D. Concannon, former Minister of State, Northern Ireland Office, in a letter sent to Charles R. Stout, US Consulate General, Belfast, 8 February 1979 (in Eilberg and Fish 1979, p. 225)*

The United States government does not recognise political prisoners of any ideology. Similar to its British ally, by categorising political offenders as 'ordinary', that is, common criminals in need of punishment, the United States views the Irish conflict in non-political terms, and thus refuses to acknowledge the political motives of republican armed struggle. A change in US policy in this regard would in fact open the door wide for domestic claims of politically-motivated offences among various groups, for example, those actions associated with the struggles of various native American and Puerto Rican groups that seek the right of self-determination for their people.

This chapter describes selected legal cases that have involved Irish republicans who have engaged in behaviour in the United States for the purpose of furthering the goal of Irish independence. Nearly all of the cases have involved weaponry transactions, namely those actions connected with the transport of weaponry for the IRA. A review of the legal cases shows that law enforcement and prosecutorial efforts that targeted Irish republicans in the United States for suspected involvement in arms transactions commenced in the early 1970s. Investigatory efforts intensified in the 1980s, with the strengthening of the US–Britain alliance.

Selected Cases

Deterring and investigating 'terrorist' activity continue to be important areas of concern for the United States government. Political offenders in the United States are often sentenced more severely than non-political offenders (Deutsch and Susler 1991; Stout and Dello Buono 1991; Susler 1995). Data have shown that the US legal system responds differently to 'terrorist' and 'non-terrorist' offenders. Smith and Damphouse (1996) compared sentence outcomes of 'terrorists and non-terrorists' who were indicted between 1982 and 1989. The authors found that 'terrorists' received significantly longer prison sentences (10 years longer, on average) than 'non-terrorists', for the same offences. In fact, politically-motivated offences served as the primary explanatory factor of lengthy sentences.

The issuance of (US) federal indictments shows some level of disparity between 'terrorist' groups and some evidence has suggested that prosecutors employ differential screening to secure an indictment. To illustrate, Smith (1993) reported data from the FBI's counter-terrorism programme for the years 1980–89. Of 28 different domestic and international 'terrorist' groups examined, more indictments (a total of 48) were issued against alleged members of 'the Order', a US-based group which seeks to establish 'white' rule, than members of any other domestic or international 'terrorist' group. The second highest number of indictments were issued against alleged IRA members (a total of 26). For comparison, one member of the Ku Klux Klan and four members of the Aryan Nations were indicted during the same ten-year period, despite the fact that members of these groups had participated in a reign of violence against US civilians during the 1980s (see Southern Poverty Law Center 1995, for evidence of violence and intimidation). No member of the anti-Castro group, Alpha 66, was indicted during this period. Comprised largely of Cuban Americans, Alpha 66 acknowledges that it seeks to 'play a determining role in the fall of the Cuban tyranny' through various means, including the provision of military training in the United States for its members (Alpha 66 n.d.). The group was funded initially by former US President Eisenhower; the Central Intelligence Agency (CIA) armed and trained group members (Gunson et al. 1991). It is not known whether these disparities are influenced by prosecutorial perceptions (or misperceptions) about the various groups. In essence, the legal system assists US allies by targeting persons who threaten those allies (Deutsch and Susler 1991).

Under United States federal law, it is illegal to provide arms to a foreign nation. Some evidence has suggested that Americans and Irish Nationals in the United States have provided arms and ammunition for the republican movement. Throughout history each major resistance in Ireland has been supported by Irish Americans, Irish Nationals in the United States and others in that country. Transactions occurred in the 1850s through to the 1920s and beyond, yet few persons in the United States were charged with crimes. In the 1970s, the Armalite (American AR-15) gained popularity among the IRA. During that time, and coinciding with the most recent presence of British troops in the north of Ireland, prosecutions of persons accused of 'gun-running' for the IRA began to increase in the United States.

Although the weaponry has become more sophisticated, there is little difference between gun-running in contemporary America and those incidents that occurred in the nineteenth century. What has changed is the official policy in the United States towards the attempts to ship weaponry from the United States for use by the republican movement. The policy change commenced in the early 1970s during the presidential term of Richard Nixon. Under his administration, the INS implemented its 'Lookout System', whereby persons entering the United States were screened for their associations with 'terrorist' activities (Celmer 1987). Further, during this time, a combined effort involving various law enforcement sectors in the United States commenced for the purpose of locating and investigating suspected IRA supporters in the United States (Clark 1977).

Fort Worth Five

In June 1972, the US Justice Department subpoenaed five men after a grand jury in Fort Worth, Texas, sought to investigate allegations of gun-running. The men, collectively known as the 'Fort Worth Five', were from New York City. All were in their seventies, born in Ireland and active in Republican circles in the United States (Wilson 1995; Holland 1999). At the hearing Paul O'Dwyer, a New York attorney, advised his clients to remain silent during questioning. By doing so, the five were charged with contempt of court and detained in jail for several months. A United States Supreme Court judge requested their release on bail in September 1972 at which time the five were released, the bail amount being raised in one night in New York bars (O'Dwyer 1979). Four months later the Supreme Court denied a writ of certiorari and the men were detained in jail again. Mounting public pressure and claims of 'grand jury abuse' contributed to a second decision by the high court to release the men (Wilson 1995, p. 93) and no indictments were ever issued.

The Bronx Case

In the 1920s, shortly after the Civil War in Ireland, Irish-born Michael Flannery immigrated to the United States. Co-founder of Irish Northern Aid, he, George Harrison (also born in Ireland), and three others were charged with arms smuggling in 1981. During the trial, Harrison testified that he had been sending weapons from the United States to the IRA for a period of 25 years. In response to the specific charges, the defendants argued that they believed that the weapons' supplier with whom they dealt worked for the Central Intelligence Agency (CIA), which sought to discourage the IRA from obtaining arms from communist countries (Wilson 1995). A jury returned a verdict of 'not guilty' and the five were released.[1] British officials were outraged at the decision and, following the verdict, the US State Department reiterated to the British government its desire to foster positive foreign relations with that country.

The Valhalla *and* Marita Ann

In 1984 crew members loaded various weaponry on board the fishing vessel, *Valhalla*, which sailed from Massachusetts to the west coast of Ireland. Crew members, including Captain Robert Andersen, John Crawley, John McIntyre, Joseph Murray and Patrick Nee, transferred the weaponry to a second vessel, the *Marita Ann*, and John Crawley joined the crew of the second vessel. Unbeknown to the crew, the vessels and the transfer of weaponry were under surveillance, after an informant had notified authorities. Authorities confiscated the weapons on board the *Marita Ann*, including over 150 firearms, 70,000 rounds of ammunition and other items. Authorities arrested John Crawley and the other crew members on board the *Marita Ann* at the time of interception. Other participants had returned to the United States on board the *Valhalla*.[2]

Controversy surfaced regarding the identity of the informant in the aftermath of the *Valhalla* incident. James 'Whitey' Bulger, described as both an IRA sympathiser and a 'long-time' FBI informant (Cullen 1997) with others helped to provide funding for the weaponry shipment. Unidentified police officers in the United States later reported that, although Bulger had helped to fund the operation, he was alleged to have notified the CIA after the ship set sail from Massachusetts. In turn, CIA agents contacted British intelligence. Bulger had allegedly received a considerable amount of money for the weaponry before the ship set sail (Cullen 1997). Other reports have indicated that IRA man Sean O'Callaghan (see Chapter 2) had informed the authorities that the weaponry shipment was heading for Ireland. O'Callaghan has admitted his informant role in this case.

John McIntyre, also on board the *Valhalla*, disappeared after he was arrested in connection with the *Valhalla* incident and then released on bail. His body has never been found. McIntyre's family and their attorney have argued that McIntyre was murdered by British agents who sought to protect the identity of the person who informed the authorities about the shipment of weaponry (Loftus and McIntyre 1989). McIntyre was portrayed in the British press as a US-based IRA informant who had notified authorities about the shipment before the *Valhalla* set sail.

Issues surrounding the identity of the informant have not been resolved. It is possible that more than one person informed the authorities. The issue raised by McIntyre's family regarding the role of the British agents involved in his death was dismissed by US authorities.

Boston 3

Collectively known as the *Boston 3*, Richard Johnson, Martin Quigley and Christina Reid were tried in Boston in 1990 for their alleged participation in the development of a radio-controlled missile system for use by the IRA. Johnson and Reid are US citizens and Quigley was an alleged member of the IRA from Dundalk, Ireland. (Two others were also allegedly involved: Eamon Maguire, an airline technician from Dublin, who left the United States prior to the arrest, and Gerald Hoy, a university instructor from Pennsylvania who pleaded guilty to the charges.)

Christina Reid is one of the few women ever to have been prosecuted in the United States in connection with attempts to assist the IRA. According to some reports Reid has Jewish American roots and changed her surname from 'Thurman' to 'Reid' in order to 'fit in' better with the Irish youth with whom she was acquainted (Adams 1989). Regarding her role in the case, she allegedly liaised for the other defendants by passing telephone messages and letters. As an adolescent she was active in the San Francisco-based republican youth organisation, Na Fianna Eireann, under the direction of Chuck Malone.[3] Malone had been convicted in 1972 for exporting weaponry to Ireland without a licence, and received two years' probation. In the 1980s he was convicted in a sting operation on charges relating to conspiracy to export weapons. His co-defendant 'turned state's evidence' and Malone was sentenced to a three-year prison term.

When the trial commenced, a US prosecutor quoted de Valera in his opening remarks in an attempt to show the south of Ireland's disdain for the IRA, perhaps thinking that the strategy would prove effective in the traditional Irish community of Boston. At the conclusion of the six-week trial, Johnson, Quigley and Reid were found guilty. Johnson was sentenced to ten years and served most of the sentence in a federal prison in Pennsylvania. Reid was sentenced to 41 months in prison and Quigley to eight years. Hoy was sentenced to only two years, a reduction in exchange for his guilty plea (Wilson 1995). Maguire was later extradited to the United States from the south of Ireland in 1994 and subsequently convicted for violating the arms export law. He was sentenced to six years' imprisonment in the United States.

Related Cases in Arizona and Florida

In 1990, Irish-born Kevin McKinley, Seamus Moley and Joseph McColgan were convicted in a federal court in Florida for conspiring to purchase a Stinger surface-to-air missile.[4] Each was sentenced to a prison term of 51 months.

During the trial, it emerged that a paid government informant had undergone psychiatric treatment in the 1980s. When questioned by defence attorneys during the trial, the informant testified that in the past he had heard voices that had instructed him to hurt himself and others. Nevertheless, his testimony served as a primary piece of evidence for the prosecution in the case.

The defendants claimed that they were entrapped by the government informant and undercover agents, i.e., that they would not have attempted to purchase the weaponry without strong government inducement.[5] The judge allowed this testimony but later instructed the jurors that they were not permitted to consider the entrapment defence. The defendants were convicted of conspiracy and acquitted of other charges. Despite their decision to convict, the jurors strongly criticised the actions and behaviours of government agents involved in the case (Rozsa and Zeman 1990).

While the defendants were detained in jail awaiting sentencing, a second government informant (also in jail) attempted to sell them another Stinger missile. Subsequently, the informant was released from jail and provided protection under the federal witness protection programme (Filkins 1991).

McKinley and Moley were indicted again in 1993 with twelve others, charged with the purchase and transport of detonators which were sent by Greyhound bus from Tucson, Arizona to New York, en route to Northern Ireland for use by the IRA. The FBI claimed that the detonators were used in various overseas explosions in 1991 and 1992. Several defendants in the Tucson case were acquitted by jury and for others charges were dropped. McKinley and Moley pleaded guilty in March 1995 and were sentenced to 19 months in prison. A third defendant, Michael 'Mixey' Martin was extradited to the United States from Britain in 1994. He also pleaded guilty and received a sentence of 16 months. For a brief time, all three men were imprisoned at the Federal Correctional Institution at Oakdale, Louisiana and each returned to Ireland after their release.[6]

Gerry McGeough

Along with Gabriel Megahey, McGeough was alleged to have attempted to purchase a large cache of arms in the early 1980s (Taylor 1997). Megahey was arrested but McGeough left the United States thereafter. McGeough was arrested in 1988 on the Dutch-German border when weapons were found in a car in his possession and spent nearly four years in a German prison without being sentenced. An arrest warrant for the attempt to purchase weaponry for the IRA was issued in 1982 in the United States, yet it was nearly ten years later (in 1991) that the US government issued an extradition warrant to the German authorities.[7] McGeough was extradited shortly thereafter and was convicted in a US District Court for conspiring to ship weaponry. He was sentenced to three years' imprisonment.

Following his extradition but before he was imprisoned in the United States, McGeough was released on bail, during which time he travelled throughout the United States and gave several speeches, all of which drew more attention to his case as well as to the Irish conflict generally. The US government spent considerable funds in their attempt to locate and extradite McGeough; the FBI, MI5 and the Irish gardaí (police) all worked together over a period of several years in their attempts to locate him. Yet McGeough subsequently served two years of the original three-year sentence. One wonders whether a three-year sentence justifies the amount of time and resources expended by the US government in trying to locate and extradite McGeough.[8]

Michael McNaught

Michael 'Micky' McNaught, originally from Derry, immigrated to the United States in the late 1980s after he learned that his name appeared on a loyalist 'hit list' (Wilson 1995, p. 235n). He and others were later arrested in an FBI sting operation for the attempted robbery of an armoured bank vehicle in Boston. A paid informant with the US government, David Ryan, had arranged details regarding the route of the armoured vehicle with McNaught's co-defendant. The informant promised that the vehicle's doors would remain open for a brief time during which the defendants could take the money. McNaught and the co-defendants claimed entrapment but this defence was not accepted by the court. McNaught was convicted in US District Court in 1991. He was transferred to Magahberry Prison in the north of Ireland in September 1997. The transfer had been requested by McNaught years earlier, and was supported by SDLP leader, John Hume, as well as government officials from the south of Ireland.

McNaught was allegedly a member of the IRA before immigrating to the United States, however his case received very little attention and only partial support from Irish America.[9] Friends in the United States, however, reported that McNaught's offence was *not* politically-motivated, that is, the attempted robbery was not intended to yield funds for the IRA. Nor was it planned on behalf of the IRA. Persons involved in the republican movement supported these claims and during his incarceration McNaught indicated that he was not in prison for political offences (personal correspondence with author, 1996). A source who was described as being 'close to the government of Northern Ireland' confirmed that the IRA were unlikely to engage in violent offences on US soil (Blake 1991). These assertions from diverse sources are probably based on fact, given the risk of loss of support from Irish America and others if violent offences on behalf of the IRA were conducted in the United States.

Father Patrick Moloney

In 1993, $7.4 million was stolen from a Brink's service depot in Rochester, New York. Charles McCormick, Sammy Millar, Father Patrick (Pat) Moloney and Tom O'Connor were among those charged with the crime. Father Moloney and Sam Millar were convicted of conspiracy to possess some of the stolen funds; a significantly large proportion of the funds, $5.2 million, was never found. Moloney was sentenced to 51 months in prison and Millar received a five-year prison sentence; the other defendants were acquitted (Wilson 1995). Although some believed that the stolen funds were destined for the IRA, the allegation was never proved in a US court.

Father Moloney was born in County Limerick, Ireland and emigrated to the United States in 1955. He is a naturalised US citizen and therefore will not be subjected to deportation upon his release from prison. He has argued his innocence since his arrest. Sam Millar was returned to the north of Ireland.

Transfers

On 1 November 1995 the south of Ireland ratified the International Convention on the Transfer of Sentenced Prisoners and some republican prisoners in the United States hoped to complete their sentences in the south of Ireland (the United States and Britain had previously ratified the Transfer Act). On the surface, the Clinton administration appeared to have 'rewarded' its republican prisoners during the ceasefire by authorising prisoner transfers to the south of Ireland: 'As a *direct result of the peace process* [emphasis added] and the continuing IRA ceasefire, the United States Justice Department moved to allow Irish prisoners to serve their sentences in Ireland' (*Irish People* 1996) and: 'In a landmark decision arising directly from the IRA ceasefire, the US Justice Department has agreed to allow Irish prisoners in the US to apply to serve their sentence in Ireland' (O'Clery 1996b).

Considerable media attention, primarily in the Irish American press, focused on the transfer of Michael 'Mixey' Martin who arrived in Dublin on 31 January 1996 to serve the remainder of his sentence in Portlaoise jail. The move was praised by the US and Irish media. In fact, Martin was scheduled to be released on 17 February so repatriation amounted to only 18 days of imprisonment in Ireland. According to one report the United States Department of Justice was responsible for the delay; allegedly six weeks were required to complete the transfer documents (*Irish People* 1996).

Kevin McKinley and Seamus Moley applied for transfer but both were released before their transfer requests had been processed. Martin Quigley and Eamon Maguire also requested transfers to the south of Ireland during the ceasefire but months before that country ratified the Transfer Act (Broderick et al. 1995). Quigley's sentence expired in December 1996 before the transfer took place. The ratification of the Transfer Act by the United States and the south of Ireland in 1995 had little impact on republican prisoners in the United States. The time involved for the application process alone, was such that release dates often occurred before the transfer could be scheduled. The public announcement of the Transfer Act amounted to no more than a symbolic gesture with little impact for the individual. Moreover, the United States' demand for transfers to Ireland was not high; eleven Irish prisoners had requested transfer to the south of Ireland as of October 1996 (Carolan 1996) and at least four of these were republicans.

British policy regarding prisoners was similar to that of the United States in that on the surface, political prisoners were 'rewarded' during the ceasefire. To illustrate, Britain re-applied the 50 per cent remission policy for political prisoners but this policy was reinstated 13 months after the IRA ceasefire was announced and only brought remission for political offences on a par with 'ordinary decent crimes'.

The south of Ireland provided early release to a large number of prisoners. From September 1994 to February 1996, the Dublin government released 36 IRA prisoners early. In December 1997 nine additional prisoners were released. However, the release policy by the Dublin government was tied directly to the ceasefires, and some scheduled releases were cancelled when the ceasefire ended in 1996. Nine prisoners, for example, were scheduled for release from Portlaoise jail in February 1996 but were denied release by Justice Minister Nora Owen after the February bombing. In fact, all nine prisoners were initially scheduled for release in December 1995 but were denied because of punishment beatings in the north (Blaney 1996).

Other Sources of Weaponry

The actual quantity of weapons, arms and funds for weaponry that reached the IRA through American sources has been widely debated. In the late 1970s, British government and RUC estimates claimed that 70 to 80 per cent of IRA weaponry came from US sources although as Wilson (1995) observed, some reports have indicated that these estimates were grossly exaggerated by the British authorities. For example, several years ago, Tugwell (1981) claimed that most of the funds raised by Irish Northern Aid were earmarked for the purchase of weaponry for the IRA. The author, however, was a one-time colonel with the British army and this might have produced a biased or misguided opinion. Despite claims to the contrary there is no evidence to date which has explicitly linked INA funds to IRA weaponry (Wilson 1994). However, over-estimating the number of weapons and funds from US sources serves the British agenda first by providing justification for the proactive responses by US law enforcement and second by discrediting Irish Americans, Irish republicans residing in the United States and persons involved with political lobbying for Irish independence. Adams (1986) claimed that over 2,000 US weapons were confiscated in Ireland between 1968 and early 1983 but noted that weaponry and funds from US sources had declined since the 1970s; by the mid-1980s, funds from the United States represented less than 5 per cent of the IRA budget, a considerable decline from the 1970s. Shannon (1993, p. 13) suggested that funds destined for the IRA from the United States have '...dwindled to the point of insignificance'.

Ultimately, there is no way of knowing the amount of weaponry and funds that have been provided to the IRA from US sources and it seems fruitless to debate the issue. No doubt weapons and funds from the United States have assisted and will continue to assist the IRA but whether Irish Americans (as opposed to other sources in the United States) have collectively contributed to the armed struggle in any *significant* way is inconclusive.

Adams (1986, p. 134) wrote: '...the enormous Irish-American population has always felt a strong sentimental attachment to the "old country" and this has been translated into a steady stream of cash and guns to the IRA'. Illicit weapon sales are very profitable yet little discussion has surfaced regarding the possibility that some US weapon suppliers have no interest at all in the Irish conflict, and instead are motivated solely by financial gain. Media and other sources, however, appear obsessed with identifying Irish Americans as the major source of weaponry for the IRA. For example, in 1993, an arms find in Belfast recovered a weapon that had been manufactured in the United States. Despite any strong evidence that suggested that the weapon had been purchased or supplied by an Irish American, an *Irish News* (1993) editorial featured the headline, 'Irish-Americans Oil the Killing Machine'. More recently, press reports highlighted the US-made weapon used by the IRA to kill a British soldier in Bessbrook, County Armagh (O'Carroll 1997). The content of the news article raised concern over 'Irish-American support for paramilitary organisations' when in fact a US-manufactured weapon does not imply that it reached Irish shores through the conscious effort of an Irish American.

Some weaponry at various times in history has been provided by American sources or purchased by the IRA with funds supplied by Americans. Wars, however, often dictate that all sides, for the most part, will seek weaponry from whatever sources are available.

The British army and the RUC are legally authorised to carry and use weaponry in the north of Ireland. Between 1969 and 1995 the RUC and the British army killed at least 357 persons in Northern Ireland (Doran 1995); the British Army has been responsible for considerably more deaths than the RUC. Most of the victims were unarmed and most were Catholics. A study that examined violent incidents that occurred in the north between 1969 and 1980 found that of the 231 people killed by security forces during those years, nearly one half (47 per cent) of the victims were Catholic civilians and 32 per cent were republican paramilitaries (White 1993). Further, disputed details have surrounded many of the killings (Asmal 1985; Jennings 1990; Tomlinson 1998). Media, however, rarely question the source of weaponry that is used in state killings.

Plastic baton rounds are used by police and army personnel allegedly to control riotous behaviour. They are not intended to kill or seriously injure, but since 1975, 14 people – half of whom were children – have died after been struck by plastic bullets fired by the British Army and the RUC (three others died after being struck by rubber bullets). All but one of the victims were Catholic. Hundreds more have suffered serious injury, including blindness and paralysis. The large number of fatalities and injuries suggests that the baton rounds are not used correctly (they are intended to be aimed at the legs at a minimum distance of 20 metres).

Prior to 1984, plastic baton rounds used by the police and army in the north of Ireland were manufactured in the United States. In that year, two victims – one who lost both eyes and a second who lost one eye – addressed a shareholders' meeting of the US manufacturer. Shortly thereafter the company ceased its trade with the British government, at least in terms of the bullet's use in Northern Ireland (personal communication, United Campaign Against Plastic Bullets, November 1996).

Plastic baton rounds are still used by military and police in Northern Ireland. Over 5,000 plastic bullets were fired during nationalist demonstrations over a three-day period in 1996. During that time, considerably fewer rounds were fired upon loyalists despite their destructive efforts that produced mayhem in Northern Ireland as a result of the Drumcree stand-off that year (American Protestants for Truth About Ireland 1996a). In a statement issued in February 1999, the Northern Ireland Minister reported that alternatives to plastic bullets were not effective so the use of plastic bullets would continue (RTE 1999). Medical authorities and human rights organisations have expressed widespread condemnation of their use (Irish National Caucus 1993; United Campaign Against Plastic Bullets 1996). The current manufacturer of the plastic rounds is not known although it is possible that another US company is the source. During one of the daily press briefings from the White House, and just after the RUC had unleashed thousands of plastic bullets upon Nationalists, Clinton's representative was asked about the White House opinion on plastic bullets. The speaker stated that '...we don't prejudge the techniques [the RUC have] used, we don't believe we're in a position to render judgment' (Office of the Press Secretary 1997a).

For several years, the British government has purchased military weaponry and other war machinery from sources in the United States. Hundreds of weaponry transactions in the twentieth century have occurred between the United States and Britain and these transactions have been fully sanctioned, if not encouraged, by the United States government. In the 1940s Britain obtained a number of destroyers from the United States and in the 1960s the United States purchased weaponry from Britain in excess of $300 million (Dobson 1995). More recently, military weapons continued to be a major trade product between the United States and Britain. Domestic export information from the United States is compiled annually by the Bureau of Census. Recent data from that source have shown that substantial amounts of arms and equipment for the British military are purchased from the United States (United States Bureau of Census 1996). During the five-year period 1991–95, the United States government authorised sales to the British government of nearly $2 million in military rifles, approximately $125,000 in military shotguns, and approximately $2.3 million in other military weapons.

During the same five-year period, the British government purchased new and rebuilt military helicopters worth $113 million from United States' manufacturers. British army helicopters are used in the north of Ireland for surveillance purposes, particularly in Catholic areas where they hover above neighbourhoods for extended periods of time in an effort to monitor homes, businesses and the movement of persons. Military ammunition and heavy equipment such as tanks also are purchased from US manufacturers for use by the British military (personal communication, US Department of State, October 1996). Additionally, the United States has authorised sales to Britain of military support equipment. For example, some high intensity searchlights used on helicopters have been manufactured in the United States and used by the British army in the north of Ireland (Dewar 1987). At one point files containing detailed information (for example, movement patterns, descriptions of the inside of homes) of a large number of the population were stored on machines that were manufactured in the United States (Wright 1978). Further, the (US) National Security Agency was alleged to have been involved in the secret wiretapping of private telephone conversations in the United Kingdom (Wright 1978).

Writers have noted that President Jimmy Carter, with the influence of the congressional Ad Hoc Committee on Irish Affairs, allegedly stopped the sale of weapons from the United States for use by the RUC. Cronin (1987, p. 317) reported, however, that years after Carter's term in office had ended, the weaponry sale was 'still under review' by the US Department of State. It is not known whether US-manufactured weapons are currently used by the RUC yet support for the RUC by the United States government is extended in other ways. For instance, RUC Chief Constable Ronnie Flanagan received special training in the FBI National Academy and subsequently lectured on intelligence gathering there (Pat Finucane Centre 1997). Other RUC officers have also trained at the FBI Academy (Royal Ulster Constabulary 1995).[10] In October 1996, this author had incorrectly assumed that RUC officers had participated in the FBI's International Training programme and contacted that branch to inquire about the training of RUC officers. During conversation with training staff there, the author did not discuss the RUC's history. The staff member with whom the author spoke reported that RUC officers had not trained in that section and without further questioning from the author the staff person reported, 'I doubt we would train officers from other countries who had engaged in human rights violations.' The statement was interesting in that the staff member appeared to have no idea that RUC officers had received training from the main FBI Academy in the previous year. Elsewhere, 'co-operation' between the FBI and the RUC in fighting the IRA has been described as 'excellent' (Ridgeway and Farrelly 1994).

History shows that the United States has provided proactive support to the British military and the RUC in the north of Ireland and continues to do so today. Yet no mention has been made of the manufacturing source of the many weapons that have been used by the military to kill civilians in the north. And no mention is made of US training provided to foreign law enforcement officers who represent an agency that has been found to be sectarian (Ellison 1997). The US and British media remain uninterested in or perhaps unaware of these transactions. It is possible that other media, for example those sources that are more sympathetic to a republican ideology, are aware of but choose to not highlight the source of British military weaponry. To do so might risk the very minor support that the US government provides to Sinn Féin.

In the north of Ireland, the terms 'troubles' and 'conflict' are misnomers. 'War' is the more appropriate descriptor and each side of the war seeks to obtain weaponry from whatever source will provide.[11] Pragmatically, there is no difference between the source of United States weaponry – be it individuals or government. Legally, however, the US government sanctions the purchase of weaponry by Britain to foster its relationship with Britain and to build its own domestic economy (in 1995, the United States led the world in arms exports with 49 per cent of the market totalling $15.6 billion; Britain was second with $5.2 billion of the world exports (United States Arms Control and Disarmament Agency 1998)). The United States cannot be regarded as a neutral participant in the Irish peace process when it supplies weaponry, other war machinery, and training to one side of the war yet condemns the other side for doing the same.

Weaponry transactions (or sanctions of) and the reciprocity that precedes or follows are important dimensions of foreign relations. When Argentina was invaded by Britain in 1982, the United States provided weaponry to Britain as well as information about Argentinean military strategy (Dobson 1995). In turn, Britain has supported the United States in its attacks on Iraq.

Government sanctions represent an important tool of foreign relations. For instance, in 1937 the United States ceased all weapon shipments to Spain during its civil war (Kittrie and Wedlock 1986). More recently, the State Department has prohibited US weaponry sales to the military and police in South Africa (US Department of State 1995). The US government provides funds at times to foreign nations in order to assist impoverished persons residing within those countries. The Amendment to the US Foreign Assistance Act forbids financial assistance to governments that practice '...a consistent pattern of gross violations of internationally recognized human rights...'.

The Amendment's subjective phrase, *a consistent pattern of gross violations of internationally recognized human rights*, is problematic in that a determination of human rights violations often depends on relations between the United States and the foreign country (Lawyers Committee for Human Rights 1996a).

Public pressure can also influence trade. In 1988, United States manufacturer TransTechnology ceased its tear gas trade with Israel after reports from both Palestinians and Israelis indicated that the tear gas was linked with miscarriages and premature deaths.

Summary

This chapter highlighted several cases in which persons had been prosecuted (and often convicted) in the United States for offences connected with their support for the Irish republican movement. Prosecutions commenced in the 1970s and intensified in the 1980s. Historical information reviewed in Chapter 1 indicated that a number of individuals and groups were involved in similar weaponry transactions during the nineteenth century, yet during that time the US government did not target Irish republican supporters for prosecution. There are few differences between nineteenth century and contemporary supporters who have supplied arms for use by the IRA. Their motives and goals are similar, although the weaponry of today is more sophisticated. The differences focus on the larger issues, such as the relationship between the United States and Britain, that has indeed become 'special'. Prosecutions by the US government are a reaction that derives in part from the alliance. Additionally, the emergence of the Provisional IRA during this time represented a significant threat to the British government, and in turn, its ally (this issue is discussed in greater detail in the conclusion).

5

Media Caricatures

'Imagine, for instance, how valuable it would be to the
Palestinian or Irish nationalist causes if their main
movements could successfully shake the label of terrorist
or how disabling it would be for the CIA to be routinely
degraded by being described as a terrorist organization.'
Falk (1988, p. 27)

A large body of research has examined the media portrayal of
social phenomena. Issues such as crime and drugs, for
example, have periodically been misrepresented or
exaggerated by the media (Barlow, et al. 1995; Hollywood
1997). US media reports are selective, and generally do not
present arguments or interpretations from competing perspectives; rather, the US media tend to '...favour certain
views and certain representations of reality over others' (Said
1997, p. 49). Further, mainstream media[1] have a tendency to
portray news in a manner that reflects the official views of
government (Chermak 1997). Herman (1982) concluded that
US media reports of foreign events are perhaps even more
likely to reflect the views of the US government. To illustrate,
he noted that State Department staff who disagreed with the
US policy on El Salvador wrote that media reports from that
area reflected the official US line and were flawed.

News reports, biased or not, have the potential for
influencing public opinion which in turn can affect or justify
public policy, regardless of whether that policy is misguided.
Herein lies the problem. False perceptions of increases in
crime, for example, when fuelled by the media, have led to
greater public support for stringent poicy on crime (Hickman
1982). Moreover, the media can influence public opinion,
particularly on topics about which the audience, for the most
part, is ignorant.

Edward Said (1997, p. 169) argued that media accounts of foreign events are influenced both by journalists' interpretations and by editors' decision-making so that media coverage of foreign issues does not necessarily represent 'knowledge'; rather, coverage represents 'interpretation'. Writer Stephen Rosenfeld (1997) of the *Washington Post* recognised this bias with regards to the Irish conflict: '…Britain's close ties to America have unquestionably won London the benefit of many unexamined doubts on the Irish issue. In any complex foreign quarrel, the American press, which is not an instrument of magic, is fair game.' Over the last three decades, the media in the United States have addressed various issues relating to the Irish conflict. For the most part, non-coverage has not been the problem – 'war news' from Northern Ireland has been reported in the United States since 1969 (Holland 1999). The problem lies with the images that are conveyed, the terms and descriptions that are used and the interpretation of events that favour one view over others. These issues are the focus of this chapter.

The British Line

Historically, the US media have favoured the British interpretation of events in relation to the Irish conflict. Press reports that addressed the Easter Rising, for example, tended to be either 'hostile' towards the Irish leaders or viewed the event as of little significance in obtaining the goal of Irish independence (Tansill 1957, pp. 202–3). An editorial in the *New York Times* was so negative with regards to the Irish participants '…it might well have been penned in London' (O'Hanlon 1998b, p. 170).

Most of the major US newspapers were very critical of Roger Casement's involvement in the uprising. After Casement was sentenced to death, news media in the United States urged that the sentence be commuted to life imprisonment. However, leniency was sought by the media only because of the belief in Casement's 'insanity' (Hartley 1987, p. 79). Many of these views portrayed in the US media were influenced greatly by the British Foreign Office (Hartley

1987) and also reflected the official policy of President Wilson's administration at the time.

The British media in Northern Ireland are 'oriented towards the views of the powerful' (Miller 1994, p. 154). The British media serve as the gatekeepers to information from Northern Ireland, influencing the ways in which stories are told to the world as well as the perceptions of the social, legal and political context in which the stories occur. With respect to the Irish conflict, more often than not the mainstream media in the United States have misinterpreted or misrepresented events, consciously or otherwise. The US media rely heavily on the British media and the British Information Service as the primary sources of news from Northern Ireland (Curtis 1984). The British government is interested in 'getting its views across' in the United States and spends millions of dollars in this endeavour (O'Hanlon 1998b, p. 182). When reporting on the Irish conflict, foreign-based news correspondents from the United States more often than not have conducted journalistic investigations and written the stories '...on the desks of various London bureaus' rather than from Ireland itself (O'Hanlon 1998b, p. 171).[2] In so doing, the US media tend to report the British version of events, that is, the official line on the political conflict. Other studies have found that journalists are concerned about maintaining their access to sources of news, and therefore are not likely to question the accuracy of information provided by those sources (Chermak 1997).

The media both control and shape the readers' views of Northern Ireland. It happens with the subtle descriptions of placenames (Thomas 1991) whereby the US media have tended to describe areas with names favoured by the British, for example, Londonderry rather than Derry[3] (see for instance, Barbash 1997; Clarity 1997), Ulster rather than the north of Ireland or the Six Counties (see for instance, *Chicago Tribune* 1997; Clarity 1997; *Los Angeles Times* 1998) or worse, 'Ulster *Catholics' (New York Times* 1997a). It happens with the choice of phrase that is used to describe a conflict-related death (Taylor 1996); the use of the words 'murder', 'assassination', or 'killing' depends in part on the interpretation of the events, and, equally important, the status of both the 'offender' and 'victim'. And it happens with the information that is released or made available to US journalists. Censorship, for example, is one factor that affects international news coverage in the US media (Lent 1977). After the Easter Rising of 1916 the British government attempted to censor news reports in the United States by screening the details and then generating its own version of the rebellion (Hartley 1987). More recently, writers have discussed the informal and formal media censorship policies in Northern Ireland that have operated for the past three decades.[4] For example, Moloney (1991) noted that in the 1970s and 1980s, media gatekeepers 'interfered' with several programmes, namely those that reflected republican views or those that highlighted controversy surrounding the police and army. He also noted that even before a government ban was introduced, the media in Northern Ireland and in Britain informally censored interviews with members of paramilitary organisations. Interviews with IRA members were screened by the Director General of the BBC but initially, selective screening was not practised with loyalist paramilitaries (Curtis 1984). A government ban was introduced in 1988 that applied to interviews and statements on radio or television from members of eleven organisations, including some political parties (namely Sinn Féin) and from persons who supported these groups. The ban applied to both Northern Ireland and to Britain. This history of censorship has no doubt affected foreign reports of the conflict.

Mainstream US media for the most part view the British government as a neutral party in Northern Ireland (Miller 1994) whereby the British government is perceived as playing the difficult role of peacekeeper in a religious war (Holland 1999). Political violence has claimed the lives of over 3,000 people since 1969, yet these deaths are portrayed as resulting from 'sectarian conflict' only (see for example, Schweid 1997), ignoring the Irish-British dimension and also ignoring the victims of state violence. In general the US media have failed to question the role of the British government in Northern Ireland; rather, 'The arguments for the British presence had been summed up in 1969 and were never subsequently contradicted or examined in depth' (Ward 1984, p.

210). To sum up, the contextual background of the political conflict has been largely omitted from news reports in the United States.

The *New York Times*, one of the leading US and world newspapers, 'sets the agenda' for most news topics that are highlighted in the United States (O'Clery 1996a, p. 112) so that press reports appearing in that newspaper are likely to be highly influential. In January 1972, 14 Catholics were killed by British paratroopers in Derry, an atrocity that is referred to as Bloody Sunday. British military spokespersons reported that over 200 rounds of ammunition were fired upon soldiers by the demonstrators, a claim that was disputed by journalists on the scene (Curtis 1984). Hayden (1998) noted that the *New York Times* suggested that the members of the British regiment were *provoked* by demonstrators [emphasis added], a portrayal that matches the British version of events that day. Nor did other major US newspapers and periodicals hold the British Army responsible for the killings (Holland 1999). Further, because smaller locally-based newspapers in the United States select news reports and editorial perspectives from the larger newspapers and wire services (Holland 1999), for the most part they too failed to question the actions of the British Army.

Images of Ceasefire

On 31 August 1994 the Army Council of the main republican paramilitary group in Northern Ireland, the Provisional IRA, called a unilateral ceasefire, followed by a similar declaration from the Combined Loyalist Military Command on 14 October 1994. Until that time Northern Ireland had experienced over 25 years of political violence with deaths of more than 3,000 people and tens of thousands injured and imprisoned. The republican and loyalist ceasefires that commenced in 1994 marked the hopeful transition of Northern Ireland toward peace. Following a referendum held on 22 May 1998 which resulted in the vast majority of the Northern Ireland electorate voting in favour of the Good Friday Agreement,[5] the new Northern Ireland Assembly was constituted. This Assembly is charged with steering Northern Ireland through the ever-hopeful transition toward peace. Although both the Assembly and this transition are nascent, with them has come a natural expectation that the quality of life will be improved.

Several political parties are represented in the Assembly and some parties are affiliated with paramilitary groups. According to the Mitchell Principles[6] and the agreed rules of procedure for the negotiations, participation in the talks leading to the Agreement and in the Assembly itself, depend in part on party-affiliated paramilitary groups remaining on ceasefire.

During the 'peace process' journalists and news editors in the United States tended to interpret events from the British perspective so that several media accounts showed favour to the British State. The US media highlighted the fact that the IRA ended its 1994–96 ceasefire, but without a mention of the failure of the British government to move forward during the 17-month ceasefire (see for example, Clarity 1997). US-based Reuters reported that the peace process was 'stalled' because the IRA had refused to co-operate (Cornwell 1997). Further, it was the IRA and not the British government that were held responsible for ending negotiation (*Los Angeles Times* 1997). In one article a journalist reported that the termination of the 1994 IRA ceasefire was a primary contributor to the intensity of the parade situation (Barbash 1997). Sinn Féin and the IRA were still viewed as one and the same; for example, a *Washington Post* (1997) article that described Sinn Féin's entry into 'all-party' talks was described by the title, 'A Welcome to the IRA'. Missing from these news reports are the explanations for the end result, the contextual backgrounds that might serve to explain the intentions and actions of the political protagonists.

Despite the ceasefires at least two dozen people were killed by loyalists between July 1996 and April 1999 (see Table 1 in appendices). The vast majority of the victims were Catholics, who were targeted for that very reason. While the Loyalist Volunteer Force claimed responsibility for some of the deaths, claims of responsibility were not forthcoming for several other murders. Subsequently, considerable evidence emerged that several victims were killed by the Ulster Defence Association (UDA), also known as the Ulster Freedom Fighters (UFF). The UDA allegedly were on ceasefire during the time of the killings (Cusack 1998). Their affiliated political party, the Ulster Democratic Party (UDP), had a place in the 'talks'. On 22 January 1998, RUC Chief Constable Ronnie Flanagan reported that UFF members were responsible for some of the murders of Catholics that had occurred in December 1997 and January 1998. One day later the UFF issued a statement which was interpreted as confessional and indicated that the recent 'response' to 'republican aggression' was over. The Ulster Democratic Party with links to the UFF was temporarily excluded from negotiations at this time. The timing of the UFF 'confession' begs the question: would the UFF have admitted their involvement without the official statement by Ronnie Flanagan, linking them to the murders? Prior to Flanagan's report, the UFF failed to claim responsibility for the murders, preferring to practice a policy of 'no claim, no blame'. Moreover, the UDP was temporarily excluded from negotiations on 26 January 1998, but only after a horrific two-month period during which several Catholics had been killed. Following the murders of Brendan Campbell, an alleged drug dealer, and Robert Dougan, a Belfast loyalist, Sinn Féin was excluded from talks on 20 February 1998. A few days after the killings had occurred the Chief Constable Ronnie Flanagan notified the Secretary of State that the IRA had committed both murders. Specific evidence which led him to that conclusion was not released to the public. The IRA never admitted to the murders and publicly stated that their ceasefire '...remains intact' (*Irish News* 1998a). Initially, the RUC portrayed those arrested in the Dougan case as 'IRA suspects', although those arrested in the Dougan murder were not charged with IRA membership. With regards to the Campbell murder, other reports surfaced that indicated that Campbell was killed 'by one of his drugs associates' and not the IRA (Trainor 1998). This information contrasts greatly with the perceptions of the RUC. More importantly, given the attitudes of the RUC towards nationalists, can the agency provide credible analyses with respect to the alleged violence of the IRA?[7] Allegations by the RUC with respect to the perpetrators of violence are taken at face value and considered to be factual. To date, the US media have failed to provide critical commentary with regards to the public claims made by the RUC; rather, these claims are assumed to be a reflection of reality as they pertain to the Northern Ireland conflict.

In the 1970s the UDA was a legal organisation in the eyes of the British government. Although violent actions by the UDA against Catholics were considerable, its role in the dozens of assassinations of Catholics was officially concealed because it operated under a different name, thereby maintaining its legal status and thus its access to press and government (Curtis 1984; Holland 1999). More recent reports have suggested that the use of 'cover names' continues among some loyalist paramilitary groups (Doherty 1999). That practice serves to operate as a flag of convenience by allowing the group to continue its violent practices but under a different name, so as to secure a place in the negotiations for its affiliated political party. Equally important, prisoners of groups that maintain their ceasefire are able to take part in the early release scheme as part of the Agreement, resulting in major reductions in time served in prison.

Following the murders of several Catholics at the hands of loyalists, McKinney (1997) addressed the issue of an alleged loyalist ceasefire in the *Philadelphia Inquirer*. He argued that '...no journalist has the guts and/or inclination to challenge' it. In fact, well after the murders of Sean Brown and several others, news media in Ireland and elsewhere reported that the loyalist ceasefire was still intact. For example, news reports in June 1997 stated that there were 'concerns' over the status of the loyalist ceasefire (Simpson 1997a) and referred to the 'crumbling' ceasefire (Simpson 1997b), as if it had never been broken, even though loyalists had killed Michael McGoldrick the previous year, John Slane in March 1997 and three victims (Robert Hamill, Sean Brown and Gregory Taylor) just prior to these news reports. Security officials were 'assessing the state of the loyalist ceasefire' (Connolly 1997) on the same day that a loyalist list of republican murder targets was discovered (Anderson 1997).[8] In late June of the same year, a leaflet was distributed in loyalist areas of Belfast. The leaflet stated:

> The loyalist people of the Village/Donegal Road have
> tolerated long enough, the nationalist scum that have
> flooded the area in recent years...as from 12 noon on the
> 1st July 1997 the loyalist people of the Village/Donegal
> Road will no longer be able to guarantee the safety of any
> Nationalist who chooses to remain within the area, nor
> can they guarantee the safety of any property where
> Nationalists are dwelling.

Catholics who resided in the area were warned to leave within
a week, yet despite these threats, police, army and the media
continued to insist that the loyalist ceasefire was still intact.

US officials and the media reacted similarly. On 9 January
1998, Senator Edward Kennedy delivered the Tip O'Neill
Memorial Lecture at Magee College in Derry. He spoke
eloquently and with passion, encouraging members of the
audience to continue the quest for peace. He promised that
Irish America would continue its commitment to 'all the
people of Northern Ireland'. Yet despite the murders of
several Catholics by loyalist paramilitaries during the weeks
and days just prior to his address, he failed to mention these
incidents at all and, in fact, praised the Unionist leadership
for their 'efforts to maintain' the loyalist ceasefire.

Media Distortions of the Perpetrators of Violence

Several years ago Curtis (1984) argued that IRA violence was
much more likely to be highlighted in the British media than
other forms of violence. Similarly, IRA violence has been the
focus of articles that have appeared in articles and books
written largely for an academic audience. In what has been
described by its US publisher as the 'authoritative resource on
terrorist groups', a book authored by Builta (1995) devoted a
number of pages to IRA violence and a brief one-page
description of loyalist paramilitaries with the soft heading,
'Ulster Movement'. The author included several years worth
of IRA activity but noted only two activities of members of
the 'Ulster Movement' both of which occurred in 1993: 1)
the killing of seven Catholics at Greysteel; and 2) the fact that
weapons were seized in England en route to Northern Ireland
for use by loyalist paramilitaries.

The IRA are perceived as the enemy and the police and army are viewed as enemy fighters: heroes, defenders and protectors of the people. For example, Kingston (1995, p. 200) described the incident at Milltown Cemetery in March 1988 when Michael Stone threw grenades and opened fire on a crowd of mourners. Stone was '...saved by brave police officers who rescued him from the crowd'.

These portrayals suggest that the IRA represent the main protagonist in the Irish conflict. 'Normality' would return to Northern Ireland if only the IRA would end its campaign of violence.

Mainstream media in the United States, like its British counterpart, have devoted considerably less attention to loyalist or state violence. Stephen Restorick, of the British military, was killed by the IRA in February 1997 and his death was highlighted by US media. The *Chicago Tribune*, for example, featured three articles on the killing.

In June 1997, four months after the death of Restorick, two RUC officers were killed by the IRA in Lurgan, County Armagh. The deaths of Constable John Graham and Reserve Constable David Johnston received international news coverage. In the United States headlines referred to the 'hundreds' of mourners in the 'grieving town' (Montalbano 1997a). Burns (1997), writing for the (Florida) *Gainesville Sun*, noted the names and ages of the officers' children and described the words expressed by them. Greenslade (1998) noted that British media referred to the event as 'cold blooded'; an 'atrocity'. Brian Feeney (1997) argued that these deaths received considerably more state attention from both Britain and the south of Ireland than the deaths of John Slane and Sean Brown, two Catholic civilians killed within three and one months respectively of the deaths of the RUC officers. Feeney noted that senior government officials, including Prime Minister Tony Blair and Mo Mowlam, Secretary of State for Northern Ireland, voiced their criticisms of the attacks and in the south of Ireland the flag was lowered to half-mast at the garda (police) headquarters. Elsewhere, President Clinton made reference to the deaths in his daily press briefing, noting that the officers had been 'brutally murdered' (Office of the Press Secretary 1997b). And the FBI

Director offered his assistance to the RUC in helping them locate the persons who participated in the attack (Mac an Bhaird 1997c).

Yet when Gregory Taylor, an off-duty police officer was killed by a loyalist mob on 1 June 1997, 'The flag at Garda HQ was not lowered to half-mast as in the case of Constables Johnston and Graham. The secretary of state did not rush to sign publicly a book of condolences. There was no book' (Feeney 1997). Further, Clinton's interest in the death of Gregory Taylor was not forthcoming. And where were the FBI? The difference in official state reaction depends on the status of the killers, with IRA violence receiving both the greatest amount of publicity (Feeney 1997) as well as offers of assistance from US law enforcement, a move indicative of the alliance between the United States and Britain.

Violence in Northern Ireland is manifested in various dimensions and has involved a number of perpetrators, including police officers and British Army personnel, acting on behalf of the State. The police and army have killed a number of people, mostly unarmed Catholics, since 1969. These fatal shootings, however, have not been investigated thoroughly by the British government.[9] Moreover, when prosecutions do occur, the accused is treated with great leniency (Tomlinson 1998). In September 1990, Paratrooper Lee Clegg and other army personnel fired 19 bullets at a stolen car, killing the passenger, Karen Reilly. Clegg was convicted and received a life sentence, only to be released by the Northern Ireland Secretary of State after serving only two years of the original sentence. At the time of his release, Clegg was permitted to take up his army post once again. At a second trial in 1999 he was found 'not guilty' of the murder, largely because the judge claimed to be uncertain about whether Clegg had fired the bullet that killed Karen Reilly. Writers have noted that many of the victims of state violence were not members of any paramilitary group, as if victim status should determine whether or not a killing is justified. However, even when members of paramilitary groups, in particular IRA members, have been killed by the police or army, disputed circumstances have often surrounded the case. In many instances, it appears that an arrest could have been made in lieu of the killing.[10] In 1988, the Special Air Service (SAS), a secret unit of the British military, killed three unarmed IRA volunteers in Gibraltar. Seven years later that case was heard before the European Court of Human Rights, which held that the killings were unlawful and that the British government was in violation of Article 2, European Convention on Human Rights which addressed the 'right to life'. Elsewhere, the killings were described as justified: SAS personnel had acted within the limits of the law; the IRA volunteers contributed to their own deaths: 'The SAS soldiers moved in to undertake an arrest but due to movements by the terrorists suggesting that one of them was going to detonate a bomb, all three were shot dead' (Kingston 1995, p. 219). State violence in Northern Ireland is rarely highlighted by the US media. This omission is consistent with the lack of response by the US government which has failed to condemn its ally publicly when violence has occurred at the hands of the British state.

The number of cases during which people have been killed in disputed circumstances has prompted the question as to whether the police and army operate a shoot-to-kill policy. Jo Thomas (1991), a former journalist with the *New York Times* London bureau, began an investigation into the possibility of a shoot-to-kill policy in Northern Ireland. During the initial stages of her inquiry, a British official asked her to terminate the journalistic investigation. She continued and in 1985 the *New York Times* published an article in which she described new evidence relating to killings by the police and army. Within ten months of the publication, Thomas was '...abruptly ordered home'; she resigned from her post shortly thereafter. Mainstream media in the United States, she argued, ignore the very issue of a shoot-to-kill policy, lest alone take sides (Thomas 1991).

On 9 July 1997, the Loyalist Volunteer Force announced that had the Drumcree parade not been permitted to proceed through the nationalist area of Garvaghy Road, the group would have bombed the south of Ireland:

If it hadn't, you would have seen the whole of the Republic of Ireland go up. We were going to take out as many as we could. We were going to hit every major city – Dublin, Cork, Galway – with no-warning bombs. Concerts, big festivals, everything (Graham 1997).

It is doubtful that the mainstream media in the United States would have ignored the threat had it been issued by the IRA and directed against targets in England.

Media Distortions Relating to the Victims of Violence

Murders by loyalists tend to be portrayed as 'random' acts of violence (Curtis 1984). The word implies that anyone in the north of Ireland has an equal probability of becoming a victim of loyalist violence. Such is not the case. It is generally Catholics who are targeted, and primarily males. To describe these violent acts as 'random' only serves to detract from the heinousness of the offences and gives the impression that victims become so as a result of accidental misfortune.

Greenslade (1998) introduced the concept of a 'hierarchy of death' that is reflected in media coverage of the Irish conflict whereby extensive coverage is reserved for deaths of British people, killed in Britain. Deaths of members of the police force and British army occupy the second level of coverage. The third level includes civilians, killed by republicans. IRA volunteers and Sinn Féin members occupy the fourth level, and finally, those deaths that receive the *least* amount of media coverage are victims of loyalist violence.

From Table 1 (in appendices), Catholic victims of loyalist violence have included John Slane, murdered in his home in the presence of his children just one month after the IRA killed Stephen Restorick. The Slane murder failed to get a mention in the *Los Angeles Times*, the *Chicago Tribune* or other major newspapers. The murder of Robert Hamill is reminiscent of twentieth-century lynchings of African Americans by white mobs in the southern regions of the United States. Hamill, also a Catholic, was beaten by a 30-

strong loyalist mob in their infamous stronghold of Portadown. He died several days later from injuries sustained in the attack. Witnesses reported that attackers jumped on Hamill's head, and that crowd members had shouted, 'kill him, kill him, kill the Fenian bastard' (Blaney 1998). Witnesses also reported that a police landrover stood by; officers observed the attack but failed to intervene. The death of Robert Hamill was never mentioned in the *Los Angeles Times* or the *Chicago Tribune*.

Since the attack on Hamill, one person, Paul Hobson, was held for trial but found not guilty of murder. Hobson received a four-year sentence for his participation in street fighting. Charges were dropped for five other males. A judge reported that he was unable to determine whether the police had failed to intervene after witnessing the attack. A writer has questioned this reasoning:

> Despite the security cameras that have long been a feature of Portadown's main street, despite the fact that this attack was carried out by local youths in front of local police officers in what is a small town by any standards, only one person was brought before the courts, and he was found not guilty of murder because of lack of evidence (McGurk 1999).

In May 1997, Sean Brown was closing up the GAA club in Bellaghy, County Derry when he was abducted and killed by loyalists. His mutilated body was found in nearby Randalstown. After the death of Sean Brown, a writer with the *Philadelphia Inquirer* wrote: 'There seems to have been a total news blackout on the murder in this country, where neither the so-called "newspapers of record" nor the wire services carried a line on it' (McKinney 1997).

Bernadette Martin, a young Catholic woman, was murdered in Aghalee by loyalists in July 1997. She and her boyfriend, a Protestant, had visited a pub that evening and later returned to his parents' home. Bernadette, her boyfriend and her boyfriend's sister were asleep when the killer crept up the stairs, entered the bedroom and shot Bernadette. She died on 15 July. Her death was not mentioned at all in the *Los*

Angeles Times although that same paper devoted considerable news space to the IRA bomb hoaxes in England that had
occurred during the same year (see for example, Associated
Press 1997b; Montalbano 1997b; 1997c).

Although a number of Catholic civilians were murdered
by loyalists in December 1997 and January 1998, the US
media failed to highlight these cases to any great extent (see
for example, *Irish News* 1998b). Terry Enright was assassinated by loyalists on 11 January 1998 while he worked as a
bouncer/doorman at a Belfast nightclub. The murder did not
get a mention in the *Los Angeles Times*; rather, on that day
the *Times* chose instead to highlight Senator Edward
Kennedy's first trip to Northern Ireland (Montalbano 1998).
Other news reports highlighted the status of the victim,
noting that Terry Enright was a relative of Gerry Adams[11]
(*Chicago Tribune* 1998). Would the murder of Terry Enright
have been reported by the US media had he not been related
(by marriage) to Gerry Adams?

Rosemary Nelson was murdered on 15 March 1999. She
died from injuries resulting from a car bomb explosion. The
Red Hand Defenders, a loyalist paramilitary group, claimed
responsibility for the murder although information has
surfaced that has suggested that loyalist 'cover names' had
been used (Doherty 1999). Unlike other victims of loyalist
violence, her death received considerable international news
coverage largely because of her 'elevated' victim status. She
was a human rights lawyer who just months before her death
had testified before the United States Congressional Sub-
Committee on International Operations and Human Rights.
She was a wife and a mother. She was a she.

Summary

The focus on IRA activity in the US media serves an
important function in that it provides further support for the
US–Britain alliance. IRA violence is viewed as the major and
sometimes the only reason for the conflict existing in the
first place. Such portrayals serve to justify the British presence

in the north of Ireland and encourage US government support in this regard.

The US media have displayed a tendency to highlight IRA activity while ignoring violence by loyalists and by the police and army. Media reports are less inclined to report murders of Catholics, except when victim status is perceived to be 'important enough' to be 'newsworthy', for example, a female lawyer, children,[12] two friends from different religious backgrounds. The US media position reflects the Unionist perception that there are 'genuine victims of terrorism', a belief that Knox (1999, p. 12) compared with the distinction between 'deserving' and 'undeserving' poor. Several years ago, Curtis (1984, pp. 112–13) observed that the British media provided victims of republican violence with 'a human identity' whereas victims of loyalist and state violence were often 'nameless, ageless, without occupations or mourning relatives'. Journalistic accounts in the mainstream US media have tended to follow this same pattern whereby victims of loyalist aggression are for the most part, 'nameless', or fail to get any news mention at all.[13] The danger in misguided media representation is that people are influenced by news reports that they read and to which they listen. Opinions are shaped not by fact but by half-truths or a failure to provide the full picture.

The disparate media attention strikes a parallel with media coverage of victims in the United States where evidence has suggested that black victims receive considerably less media attention than whites (Smith 1984). Findings from those studies parallel results from research that examines legal processing in the United States. For example, several empirical studies conducted in the United States have shown that defendants who target black victims are treated more favourably by the legal system compared with defendants whose victims are white (Lafree 1989; Spohn 1994). This system of disparity is one that *devalues* black victims of crime. Moreover, this disparity exists in a legal system that incorporates several safeguards that afford due process for the accused (but also recognises the 'rights' of the victim). Similar safeguards and other constitutional protections are lacking in the legal system in Northern Ireland, so that the pattern uncovered in the US legal system begs the question: to what extent does Northern Ireland's legal system discriminate based on victim status? Anecdotal evidence suggests that only a handful of cases involving Catholic victims reach the courts, and further, that defendants in these cases are treated with great leniency. Since 1996, arrests have yet to take place in several of the murders involving Catholic victims of loyalist violence. Literally dozens of studies in the United States have examined the effect of offender or victim race/ethnicity on criminal justice outcomes (for example, arrest/charge, detention prior to trial, conviction/acquittal). Several studies have found that even when offence and prior criminal history are taken into account, blacks are still treated more harshly than whites in various stages of the criminal justice system (for a review of research, see Walker et al. 1996). At times, these findings have been used to shape legal policies that aim to eliminate or reduce race discrimination in criminal justice outcomes. Similar research is needed in Northern Ireland – empirical studies that examine the effect of religious background on legal processing. Researchers, however, have been denied the necessary data in the interests of 'security'. Moreover, some criminal justice authorities claim that they do not collect information on religion. This claim, however, does not dismiss the possibility that Catholic and Protestant 'offenders' and victims are treated differently by police and other formal agents of control. Even without the official collection of religious background information, criminal justice decision-makers in Northern Ireland remain part of society whereby other people's religious background is learned through several informal cues (Parker 1994). Additionally, denying researchers the access to information that is needed in order to conduct studies of legal processing only serves to foster suspicion. In the absence of scientific research in this area, we rely on impressions, tainted or otherwise. Criminal justice officials, namely the police, prosecutors and judges, as well as senior staff with the Northern Ireland Office, claim that the system is unbiased. It might better serve the interests of justice to release the data and let the findings speak for themselves.

6

The Facade of Neutrality

'Senator Gore and I share the goal of all Irish Americans for peace in Northern Ireland.' *Statement by President Bill Clinton, prior to being elected to the Presidency, (cited in O'Clery 1996a, p. 23)*

A decade ago Cronin (1987, p. 12) claimed that 'no [US presidential] administration supported Irish independence'. A review of US presidential policies in the nineteenth and twentieth centuries indeed has demonstrated that non-intervention in the Irish conflict was the acceptable policy of the executive branch. Under the leadership of President Bill Clinton, however, that policy changed somewhat. Clinton has been credited with having an interest in the Irish conflict and the search for peace in Northern Ireland (O'Clery 1996a; Holland 1999). Supporters have claimed that he has had 'a greater impact on Northern Ireland' than any of his predecessors (O'Dowd 1998). Trina Vargo (1998), former adviser on foreign policy to Senator Edward Kennedy, noted that '...it cannot be assumed that, 15 years from now, the Irish American agenda – whatever it is at that time – will automatically enjoy the priority in American foreign policy that it does today with the Clinton administration...'.

This chapter addresses the issues of a) whether President Clinton prioritised the 'Irish problem' and b) the extent of his commitment to finding peace.

The Clinton Era

President Clinton's involvement in the north of Ireland has vacillated in his attempts to appease both Britain and Irish America, a formidable but impossible task. With regard to the MacBride Principles[1] Clinton initially voiced approval but in April 1996 he vetoed the Foreign Affairs Authorization Act that incorporated these guidelines (reportedly for other reasons; see O'Hanlon 1996b). He again endorsed the MacBride Principles at the Democratic National Convention during the summer of 1996.

Clinton was the first president ever to visit the north of Ireland during a term, although several of his predecessors were born in or had ancestors from Ireland. His visits and his appointment of George Mitchell to chair the 1996 'peace negotiations', were greeted with considerable support by Irish America and also sanctioned by the British government. Jean Kennedy Smith, Ambassador to the south of Ireland under Clinton's administration, visited the north on several occasions. At one point, she observed the proceedings of a Diplock court, a striking difference from her predecessors who rarely travelled to the north at all (O'Clery 1996a). Congressional hearings on Northern Ireland, banned since 1972, took place under the Clinton administration. Congressman Ben Gilman, one of the strongest congressional supporters of issues pertaining to the north of Ireland, was named chair of the International Relations Committee in 1994. Under his guidance, a congressional hearing on Northern Ireland was held in 1995, followed by a second hearing on human rights in Northern Ireland in June 1997. One month before the June hearing, congressional hearings were held on issues pertaining to the political deportees during which several members of Congress voiced their support.[2] In April 1999, the International Relations Committee, US House of Representatives, held hearings on policing in Northern Ireland.

Perhaps Clinton's strongest decision was to grant a visa to Gerry Adams, the first Sinn Féin representative to be provided with a visitor visa in 20 years.[3] Adams' first visa was granted in 1994 (before the IRA ceasefire) and despite strong opposition voiced by the British government, Clinton was encouraged by Irish Prime Minister, Albert Reynolds and by Ambassador Jean Kennedy Smith (O'Brien 1995). Adams was provided with another visa in 1995; since then he has visited the United States on several occasions and has been permitted to raise funds and establish an office in Washington, D.C. ('Friends of Sinn Féin'). In 1997 its representative, Mairead Keane, attended President Clinton's state of the union address, a prestigious affair in Washington circles. She also was the invited speaker at the United States Naval Academy. These events indicate that in the United States Sinn Féin was acknowledged, represented and viewed as a respectable political party. Between March 1995 and December 1997 contributions to the Friends of Sinn Féin totalled $2.3 million (O'Hanlon 1997b). The granting of approval to Sinn Féin to raise funds in the United States has no doubt assisted the political party in meeting expenses. Equally important, the policy is highly symbolic in that it provides legitimacy and credibility to the party.

Clinton's decisions led to harsh criticism by Britain and pro-British supporters in the United States and temporarily affected the US–Britain alliance. Kennedy Smith was painted as an advocate of the IRA for her support of the Adams' visa. She also helped to secure a visa for former prisoner and IRA leader, Joe Cahill, who had previously been deported from the United States in 1971 and 1984 (Guelke 1996). The criticisms were voiced by Raymond Seitz, United States Ambassador to Britain in the early 1990s, who objected to any involvement at all in Northern Ireland by Kennedy Smith. Presidential hopeful Bob Dole also criticised Clinton for granting a visa to 'terrorist' Gerry Adams[4] (Fletcher and Rhodes 1996). Former Prime Minister John Major was outraged. By 1995, the term 'special relationship' was banned in the British Embassy in Washington, D.C. (O'Clery 1995). Speaking at the (US) Republican National Convention in August 1996, former Secretary of State James Baker announced that relations between the United States and Britain were the worst since the War of Independence. A London *Times* (1997) editorial demanded that 'Washington needs to move much closer to the stance taken by London and Dublin if it is to have any positive part in the post-Docklands peace process'.

The previously soured relationship began to mend in 1997 with the newly elected British Prime Minister, Tony Blair. In May of that year, Blair 'honoured' Clinton by inviting him to the meet with the British Cabinet – the second time in history that a US president was provided with this opportunity. Blair's invitation was an important symbolic gesture, and suggested that the relations between the US and Britain were improving quickly. Clinton extended his visit in England so that he could '…spend more time cementing his personal friendship with Tony Blair' (*Irish News* 1997b). By 1998 Clinton provided full '…support of British policy in Northern Ireland' and Blair extended his support to Clinton in light of the 'sex scandals' (Murphy 1998). In fact, on the basis of Britain's support for the US invasion of Iraq and Blair's offer of sympathy to Clinton over allegations concerning his personal behaviour, Blair hoped that Clinton would continue to assist him with issues relating to Northern Ireland (MacLeod 1998). Reciprocity was well on the way. Although Clinton's commitment to Northern Ireland was a fresh change from the long history of presidential non-intervention with regards to the Irish conflict, Clinton's position squarely mirrored Blair's. The United States was in no way a neutral outside observer.

Human Rights and Foreign Policy

Despite brief periods of strain, the alliance between the United States and Britain has strengthened considerably during the twentieth century. In recent decades foreign policy considerations have become increasingly more salient than human rights concerns yet, as some have argued, governments in fact violate human rights when humanitarian refugees are returned to the country of origin (Hailbronner 1988). Despite the dissemination of international standards of human rights, the United States has at times applied different standards depending on its relationships with governments of foreign countries. This argument is best illustrated from information contained in the US State Department's *Country Reports on Human Rights Practices*, published annually since 1976.

The *Country Reports* are intended to describe the type and extent of human rights abuses in those countries that receive US assistance and in member countries of the United Nations. Information is collected from foreign government officials, their military, human rights organisations and academics, among others, and is collated by US embassy staff who prepare draft reports. It is not known precisely what information is excluded by embassy staff. Moreover, the State Department edits the drafts prepared by embassy officials and again, it is not known what information is excluded at this second stage of screening.

Warren Christopher, former US Secretary of State for the Clinton administration, claimed that the *Country Reports* represent an 'impartial' description of human rights violations 'that might otherwise be covered by the veil of indifference' (Scherr 1997, p. 1). Impartiality, however, differs by country and more specifically, by the nature of the relationship between the United States and the foreign government to which a particular report refers.

For several years, the Lawyers Committee for Human Rights (LCHR) has published its critique of the *Country Reports*. In its critique of the 1995 *Report*, the Committee argued that State Department reports of human rights' violations are affected by foreign relations: 'U.S. allies, at times, are not held overtly responsible for human rights violations' (Lawyers Committee for Human Rights 1996a, p. 3). And citing examples from Israel, the LCHR has suggested that 'international human rights norms can be compromised when larger political goals are at stake' (Lawyers Committee for Human Rights 1996a, p. 4).

The State Department reminds its embassies that similar criteria must be used when reporting violations by government allies and dissenting groups. However, the LCHR argues that different standards of proof are applied to allies. Using Northern Ireland as an illustration, the Committee noted that 'violations by paramilitaries are invariably presented as hard fact; violations by the [friendly] state are presented as "claims", "allegations", or "reports" (1996a, p. 4). Several examples of this argument can be found in the 1996 *Country Reports on Human Rights Practices: The United Kingdom,* section on Northern Ireland. Harassment of citizens by security forces (police and army) was described in terms of 'accusations' (p. 5). Commenting on the Drumcree crisis for that year, the *Country Report* noted that 'Irish Nationalists argue that the RUC reacted more aggressively and vigorously to quell nationalist disturbances than toward loyalist lawbreakers' (p. 2). The *Country Report* presented this police practice of excessive force as a nationalist 'claim' rather than as a 'fact'. During the 1996 Drumcree crisis police fired 5000 plastic bullets at nationalists during demonstrations over a four-day period compared, with 662 plastic bullets fired during the five-day unionist demonstration (Amnesty International 1997) yet the *Country Report* made no mention at all of the differences in the use of force by police.

The death of Dermot McShane, killed by an armoured government vehicle, was stated to have occurred during 'street fighting' (p. 3) rather than during a demonstration. Moreover, the *Country Report* described McShane as a 'convicted Republican terrorist' (p. 3), as if a person's previous status determines whether s/he is worthy of the label, 'victim'. Labelling as such gives the impression that the victim somehow contributed to his death. Portrayals of 'victim-precipitated behaviour' serve to justify or excuse the behaviour of the police.[5]

The *Country Report* stated that 'Freedom of worship has been legally guaranteed to members of all faiths and denominations' (1997, p. 10) yet, curiously, there was no mention at all of the Catholic worshippers in Harryville who withstood loyalist jeers and verbal abuse as they made their way to mass each Saturday evening. The loyalist demonstration began in mid-1996 and ended just over 42 weeks later after the local priest felt he needed to cancel Saturday evening mass. The evening worship began again two months later and the loyalist protest outside the Catholic chapel began again shortly thereafter.

US Support for Violations of Due Process

Comparisons between the legal systems of Northern Ireland and the United States are striking. The criminal justice system in Northern Ireland is allegedly designed to 'preserve security' but at a great sacrifice to individual liberty. In the United States, constitutional protection requires that in most cases, arrests can be made only when a police officer has probable cause to believe that: 1) an offence was committed; and 2) the individual in question committed the offence. For 'terrorist' offences, 'reasonable suspicion', a much lower standard than probable cause, is used in Northern Ireland. Specifically, an arrest can be made when an officer has a reasonable suspicion that a person has engaged in the commission, preparation or instigation of terrorism. Such arrest powers are substantial. Data have shown that most arrestees in the north are never charged with an offence. During the four-year period 1985–88, the percentage of arrestees who were charged with an offence ranged from 3 per cent to 17 per cent (Northern Ireland Office 1989). These extensive arrest and detention powers continue today despite strong recommendations for their repeal. Critics have argued, for example, that the arrest powers infringe the right of individual freedom and liberty and have questioned why they have not been repealed, particularly during a lengthy ceasefire period (Lawyers Committee for Human Rights 1996b).

In the north of Ireland, persons prosecuted for scheduled [political] offences[6] are tried in Diplock courts – at which juries are *not* used; rather one judge presides at trial. This court system would be unacceptable in the United States where defendants have a constitutional right to trial by jury. Scholars have concluded that by extraditing IRA members – alleged or otherwise – the United States government extends its approval of the Diplock courts (Iversen 1989). Additionally, by subjecting Irish former political prisoners to the threat of deportation, the United States government places great credence in the legal process by which these persons were arrested, prosecuted and convicted. In effect, the United States provides *de facto* support for legal proceedings that have been criticised by several international human rights organisations. Liberty, a Britain-based organisation that works to defend human rights and civil liberties, reported in the early 1990s that of 100 suspected cases of miscarriages of justice, approximately one quarter involved Irish prisoners (reported in Borland et al. 1995, p. 384).

Criticisms voiced by other human rights organisations have focused on:

- police intimidation and harassment of lawyers (United Nations Human Rights Commission 1998)
- detention without sufficient cause (Human Rights Watch/Helsinki 1991)
- excessive detention of seven days in some cases, without charge (Lawyers Committee for Human Rights 1996b)
- psychological or physical abuse during police interrogation (Committee on the Administration of Justice 1993; European Committee for the Prevention of Torture 1993; Human Rights Watch/Helsinki 1994; United Nations Human Rights Commission 1995)
- lack of safeguards during police interrogation and detention (Amnesty International 1997)
- convictions based solely on uncorroborated testimonial evidence (Amnesty International 1991; Human Rights Watch/Helsinki 1993)
- trial use of informants who lack credibility (Amnesty International 1988)
- non-jury (Diplock) trials without regard for defendants' preference (United Nations Human Rights Commission 1998; Lawyers Committee for Human Rights 1996b)
- inference of guilt drawn about persons who choose to remain silent (Amnesty International 1993; Lawyers Committee for Human Rights 1996b; United Nations Committee Against Torture 1995)
- failure of police to apply fairness (Amnesty International 1997)
- police use of excessive force (Human Rights Watch/ Helsinki 1997).

Additionally, for several years the United Nations has received reports of harassment and intimidation of defence attorneys in Northern Ireland. Those reports prompted the official visit by the United Nations' Special Rapporteur on the Independence of Judges and Lawyers in 1997. One preliminary statement issued by the UN lawyer was a call for a complete inquiry into the assassination of Patrick Finucane by loyalist paramilitaries in 1989. Finucane, a human rights lawyer, was shot and killed in his Belfast home in the presence of his wife and family. At the time of his death he was one of the few lawyers in the north of Ireland who defended persons accused of politically-motivated offences. No arrests have ever been made. For several years, however, allegations have surfaced suggesting that the security forces and loyalist paramilitaries colluded to murder Finucane. An alleged British Army double agent was said to have accompanied loyalists to Finucane's home in preparation for the murder (Maloney 1998). Other evidence has surfaced that suggests that the RUC allegedly had knowledge of the planned murder but failed to intervene (McKinney 1999). Human rights lawyer Rosemary Nelson was killed by loyalist paramilitaries in March 1999 when a bomb exploded under the car that she was driving (see also Chapter 5). Prior to her murder, she testified before the US Congress during which she described the abuse and intimidation she received from the RUC. For example, she spoke of incidents whereby RUC officers had threatened her physically, engaged in sectarian harassment and directed abuse towards her. She had served as legal advisor to Sean McPhilemy. author of *The Committee: Political Assassination in Northern Ireland* (1998). She also represented the residents of Garvaghy Road. Her clients included the family of Robert Hamill, for whom she had filed a civil suit against the police for their failure to intervene in the fatal beating. United Nations' Special Rapporteur Param Cumaraswamy reported after her death that he had warned the British government about his fears for Nelson's safety on several occasions over a period of two years (Gray 1999). The RUC sought to lead the murder investigation into her death and the FBI London office supported this idea. These events are noteworthy and bear repeating: a lawyer testified before United States congressional members that local police had threatened her, harassed her and abused her verbally and physically. A United Nations' Special Rapporteur had reported his concerns for her safety. She was subsequently murdered and the police force that had threatened, intimidated, harassed and abused her wanted to lead the investigation. London-based FBI Special Agent John Guido, who at first offered his assistance to the RUC investigation, later withdrew his support claiming that he had been 'greatly impressed' by the work of the RUC (Doherty 1999). Local and international response has been to call for an independent inquiry into her murder. Several human rights groups, the United Nations and the US House of Representatives, among others, have called for an independent inquiry and investigation. The Human Rights Sub-Committee of the United States House of Representatives passed a resolution which called for the RUC to be barred from participating in the murder investigation. Some reports, however, have indicated that the US State Department attempted to hinder its passage (Carroll 1999).

The United States government fails to consider that nearly every aspect of the legal system in the north of Ireland violates due process under United States law. Over 40 years ago Britain ratified the European Convention on Human Rights and Fundamental Freedoms but to date has yet to incorporate the protections into its own laws, thus, human rights are not guaranteed in Britain. Violations of human rights can be reviewed by the European Human Rights Commission but the process is expensive (*New York Times* 1997b). By 1997, Britain was second only to Italy in the number of times it had breached the Convention (*Irish People* 1997). One notable decision (described in Chapter 5) involved the 1987 killings of three unarmed IRA volunteers by the Special Air Service (SAS) in Gibraltar whereby the European Court of Human Rights in Strasbourg found the British government to be in violation of the European Convention on Human Rights.

The Clinton administration has been made aware of human rights abuses in the north of Ireland (see Committee on the Administration of Justice 1994). For example, during his first presidential election campaign, Clinton acknowledged 'collusion between the security forces and Protestant paramilitary groups' (cited in O'Grady 1996, p. 3). Further, the section on Northern Ireland from the *Country Reports on Human Rights Practices* has shown that the US Department of State has documented allegations of abuse of detainees (1997a, p. 5; 1996, p. 1), acknowledged a United Nations report that requested that Castlereagh holding centre be closed 'as a matter of urgency' (1996, p. 1), noted criticisms regarding the denial of immediate legal assistance for persons detained (1996, p. 1) and acknowledged those criticisms regarding the right to silence (1997a, p. 8; 1996, p. 1). The State Department document also reported allegations of collusion between loyalist paramilitaries and members of the security forces (1996, p. 1), mentioned the large number of disputed deaths by members of the security forces (1996, p. 3) and reported criticisms regarding the standard for use of deadly force (1996, p. 3). Perhaps the strongest statement issued in these reports is that 'Special "emergency" restrictions affect due process' (1997a, p. 8). In sum, the United States government seeks to return several Irish republicans to the very legal system that it has recognised to be discriminatory. Proactive attempts to initiate peace through ceasefire did not affect United States government policy regarding Irish republicans in the United States; rather, foreign policy and the 'special relationship' have dictated the treatment of individuals.

Terrorist List

The Antiterrorism and Effective Death Penalty Act of 1996 provided the Secretary of State with the authority to determine a list of foreign terrorist organisations.[7] Criteria for list designation are unclear, at least to the observer, although a 'threat to US interests' may be one factor that determines whether a group is designated 'terrorist'. Generally, the list operates for two years, at which time the information is reviewed and modified if deemed necessary. However, the Secretary of State has the authority to add and remove groups from the list at any time (groups can also be deleted from the list through congressional legislation).

For most of 1997 the IRA was included on the list whereas loyalist groups were excluded. The implications for being placed on the list are that: 1) members of the group are ineligible for visas, including visitor visas; 2) groups are not permitted to raise funds in the United States; and 3) persons who provide funds or other support to designated groups are in violation of federal law and are subject to a maximum ten-year prison sentence (United States Department of State 1997b).[8] The State Department removed the IRA from the list in October 1997 in an effort to provide an incentive for peace. O'Hanlon (1997c) suggested that fundraising in the United States by Sinn Féin would have been curtailed by the United States government had the IRA continued to be on the list. Unionists were outraged when the IRA was dropped form the list (McAleer 1997b) yet few Unionist politicians criticised the omission of loyalist paramilitary groups from the State Department list.

The State Department has published annual reviews of foreign terrorism, including a section on the United Kingdom. Its 1996 report focused exclusively on republican, namely IRA, violence. No mention at all was made of loyalist violence for that year. In the 1997 report, the section on the United Kingdom opened with descriptions of IRA and other republican activity. Descriptions of loyalist paramilitary actions were much briefer, consisting only of LVF activity. Although that report was for the calendar year 1997, the final sentence for the United Kingdom section describes how Sinn Féin was banned from 'all-party' talks from January to March *1998* because of IRA activity. No mention at all is made of the January 1998 murder spree by loyalist paramilitaries, events that created substantial fear and apprehension in the nationalist community. In the 1998 report, the LVF were described as '...one of Northern Ireland's most vicious' paramilitary groups, but not one victim of loyalist violence is mentioned in the report. In fact, the State Department credited the LVF for surrendering '...a cache of weapons'.

Summary

Previous US presidential administrations had claimed to be neutral with respect to the Irish conflict and, consistent with this claim they had continued with a policy of non-intervention. To be neutral, however, only serves to justify and in fact encourage the Unionist and British points of view and policies, hence the phrase, 'facade of neutrality'. President Clinton's interests in the Irish conflict clearly have gone far beyond that of his predecessors, and writers and politicians alike have recognised his efforts in this regard.

Several Sinn Féin representatives, including their leader, have been permitted to enter the United States where fundraising has also been authorised. These decisions have demonstrated that Sinn Féin is a respectable and credible political party in the eyes of the US government. However, to the IRA, Clinton has offered only 'surface rewards', for example prison transfers that have had little impact for the individual,[9] the suspension of several deportation orders for which no progress has been made in nearly two years and the removal of the IRA from the 'terrorist list' during a period of ceasefire. These decisions were highly publicised yet whether they have reflected any real incentive to the IRA in maintaining its current ceasefire remains to be seen.

Shannon (1993) argued that the United States has been and is currently committed to the dual goals of protecting human rights and fighting discrimination. President Clinton has expressed great interest in achieving peace in Northern Ireland and has shown some commitment to this end. At the same time, however, evidence from this chapter has suggested that the Clinton administration has for the most part ignored several issues relating to human rights in Northern Ireland. In light of its special relationship with Britain, human rights have become a side issue.

Conclusion

'Freedom opened her arms to receive him, and beneath the glorious banner of the United States he found a haven and a rest'. *Life of John Mitchel, Sillard (1908, p. 135)*

'But the lady's in the harbor and still I hear her song give to me all you who've suffered oppression for so long. And let it not be said that America did cry if you've come a seeking justice no Irish need apply' *Kirk M. Olson*[1]

Political Offences versus Terrorism

The issues addressed in this book arose precisely because of the US and British government distinctions between politically-motivated offences and behaviour described as terrorism. What appears to be a simple course in semantics has real implications for individuals as well as for social, political and legal policies.

Irish republican prisoners argue that their offences are politically motivated rather than 'criminal' and therefore disassociate their behaviour from crime. They do not recognise the British courts in which they were convicted and in turn they do not report past convictions when asked by the INS. When court convictions are not revealed but are subsequently discovered by the INS, persons are considered to have entered the United States by illegal means and are subject to deportation. In a similar vein, history shows that a political offence exception was firmly embedded in nearly all US extradition treaties for nearly two centuries. The United States greatly restricted the exception with the revision of its treaty with Britain in 1986. Those changes have made it more difficult for US courts to rule that actions on behalf of the Irish republican movement do indeed result from political motivations.

On the surface, the British government strongly disputes the political motivation of Irish republican prisoners yet the subtleties of its legal system show otherwise. For example, Section 66 of the Emergency Provisions Act 1991, as amended[2] defines 'terrorism' as the 'use of violence for *political* ends' (emphasis added). Moreover, the legal system in the north of Ireland, past and present, has provided *de facto* acknowledgement of politically-motivated offences. For example, some individuals who have faced deportation or extradition from the United States were in fact provided with 'special category status' during their imprisonment in the north of Ireland, precisely because their offences were politically motivated ('special category status' was used by the British government from June 1972 until March 1976). Franklin (1997) noted that the physical and social structure of Long Kesh prison, and specifically its resemblance to prisoner of war camps during the Second World War, in effect confirms the POW status of Irish republicans. Irish republicans have been and continue to be tried before special courts, where the rules are different from those reserved for persons accused of 'ordinary' crimes. If political offences do indeed constitute general crime as the two governments assert, it follows that one court with one set of legal rules should suffice. Several republican (and loyalist) prisoners have been released from prison as part of the Good Friday Agreement. As of June 1999, 273 prisoners have had their sentences reduced or have been released from prison under the Agreement. A total of 400 paramilitary prisoners are expected to be released by the end of year 2000 and these releases are tied directly to the political peace process. Persons imprisoned for other offences, for example, rape and drug trafficking, have not been included under the Agreement's prisoner release scheme. Despite these attributes of the legal system in Northern Ireland, the British government continues to utilise the label 'terrorist' rather than 'political offender'; to do otherwise would undermine the justification of the British government in the north of Ireland and encourage further international support for the Irish republican cause (Findlay 1985).

The United States, following the lead of its British ally, now views Irish political prisoners as ordinary criminals. By so doing, the objectives of and reasons for the Irish republican struggle are obfuscated rather than highlighted. The US government, however, does acknowledge the presence of political prisoners in other countries. The relationship between the United States and the foreign government, however, affects the decisions regarding whether acts are considered to be politically motivated or indicative of terrorism. On 11 December 1986 a ceremony was held at the White House in honour of international Human Rights Day. President Reagan's special guest was Armando Valladares, who had been convicted and imprisoned for 22 years in Cuba for offences related to 'terrorism' (Hamm 1991). Twelve days after the ceremony took place the Supplementary Treaty took effect, thereafter greatly reducing successful claims of politically-motivated offences among Irish republicans in the United States.

People previously labelled 'terrorists' have become respected individuals: former political prisoner Nelson Mandela is a prime example. As recently as 1990 the African National Congress was defined as a terrorist group by the US State Department. More recently, Mandela has been recognised as a political leader. The change in government perception prompted a question from congressional member Peter King to the INS General Counsel, David Martin, during a congressional ad hoc committee hearing held in February 1997: if President Mandela were to emigrate to the United States, would the INS seek to deport him on the basis of his past imprisonment?

Shift in US Policy

During the nineteenth and most of the twentieth centuries, Irish political dissidents found safe refuge in the United States. During this period the tools for exclusion, namely deportation and extradition, were not used by the US government to target Irish former prisoners. US policy regarding Irish political offenders changed dramatically beginning in the early 1970s when indictments were filed and prosecutions commenced against Irish republican supporters in the United States. Those government strategies were largely unsuccessful in the early 1970s, which prompted the US government to utilise other forms of exclusion, namely deportation and extradition.

The historical alliance between the United States and Britain continued throughout this period and at times strengthened considerably. The alliance has contributed greatly to the executive branch policy of non-intervention regarding the Irish conflict, a policy that continued throughout the 1970s and 1980s. A major component of the alliance has been the reciprocal support extended during times of war and other military conflict. Support from Britain was forthcoming during Vietnam, the 1986 attack on Libya, the Gulf War and later in the Balkans. The United States extended its support to Britain during the invasion of the Falkland Islands and also with regards to its presence in Northern Ireland.

Other factors emerged that contributed to the policy change that occurred during the United States during the 1970s and 1980s. One explanation focuses on the emergence of the Provisional IRA, whose ideology and impact differed from its predecessors.

Smith (Smith, M.L.R. 1997) analysed the strategies of the IRA border campaign of 1956 to 1962 and argued that although the campaign emphasised nationalism and 'guerrilla warfare' it lacked political goals. The intended political accomplishments of the campaign were never stated. He noted further that the campaign was largely ineffective because it was not based on a specific or clear political ideology. In the 1960s, under the leadership of Cathal Goulding, the political ideology of the IRA drifted decidedly leftwards with less emphasis on guerrilla warfare. The ideology of the 1960s was not based on Marxism per se; rather, it drew from socialist-republican history, such as that rooted in the beliefs of James Connolly and others (Smith, M.L.R. 1997).[3]

The Provisional IRA emerged in 1969–1970 and its strategy differed substantially from its predecessors of the border campaign era. Political mobilisation through careful planning as well as suggested political policies were incorporated into its overall objectives (Coogan 1995). Within this framework, its stated goal was a democratic socialist republic. Socialism in this context focused on the Irish people's right to control their own destiny, their own country (cited in Smith, M.L.R. 1997). The IRA became 'politicised' with members 'trained as socialist political soldiers' (O'Brien 1995, p. 127).

Since then several republicans including Gerry Adams have rejected and distanced themselves from a Marxist label (Smith, M.L.R. 1997). The British government, however, exploited the Marxist link with Irish republicanism and did so in order to encourage the US government to share its perception that the IRA is the enemy. The major propaganda coup is reflected in an official document prepared for the intention of 'general briefing purposes'. Drafted by the Northern Ireland Office (NIO) in conjunction with the British Foreign Office, a revised version of the manuscript was issued in August 1983.

The document suggested that foreign support for the IRA comes from Communists (among other groups): 'Sympathy for their cause is also a recurring theme in Soviet propaganda.' Linkages between the IRA and several other groups were reported, noting that the groups are 'united by various Marxist slogans'.

A major section of the NIO document linked the IRA with countries led by opposing governments of the United States. For example, in a subtle reminder of the relations between the United States and Israel, the report suggested that, 'The Provisionals have warmly espoused the Palestinians' cause.' The NIO noted an article from *An Phoblacht/Republican News*, the primary journalistic medium of the republican movement, in which a republican author voiced criticism of the supportive role of the United States when Israeli troops entered Lebanon. The bulletin went on to describe how Gerry Adams had sent a letter to the people of Grenada in support of their quest for independence. Although noting a lack of corroborative evidence, the NIO stated that IRA members were training in El Salvador and also that a meeting between former IRA prisoner Kieran Nugent and Cuban officials had reportedly been held in Denmark. The NIO document continued with a quotation from Sinn Féin representative Martin McGuinness noting that he allegedly stated that, 'Our heroes are all the people who fight for national liberation.' In response to the statement, the document inferred that McGuinness' heroes included four countries: Cuba, El Salvador, Nicaragua and Vietnam, each of which has been a thorn in the side of US foreign policy.

The British Foreign Office, from where the document was derived, is a primary source of news from Northern Ireland that is highly influential in the interpretation of events. As described in Chapter 5, the US media rely greatly on the Foreign Office for news material relating to the Irish conflict. Information from the Foreign Office has been disseminated to various non-media entities as well. The document described above, for example, was submitted to the United States Senate (1984) during its investigatory hearing into the deportation case involving Michael O'Rourke.

'Marxism' conjures up images of 'evil' for many Americans. It threatens the very structure of a capitalist economy. The portrayal of Irish republicans as Marxists served to encourage and later justify the change in US policy towards Irish republicans. In this regard, the British government acted as 'claims-maker', believed by the US because of the allied relationship. However, the Marxist portrayal represented only one of the factors that contributed to the US shift in policy. It was perhaps a 'necessary but not sufficient' condition for change. A second factor concerned the perceived strength of the Provisional IRA which represented a major threat to the British, and in turn, US interests. The IRA campaign of the early 1970s has been described as 'the greatest challenge to the continuance of the British connection in fifty years' (Bowyer Bell 1990, p. 372). The US rose to meet this challenge and supported its ally.

Support and Publicity

Throughout history, nearly every uprising in Ireland has been supported by individuals and groups in the United States. In the absence of US government intervention in the Irish conflict, support from citizens and residents in the United States has become paramount.

Support from Americans has tended to vacillate, often coinciding with major events in Ireland. For example, the executions that followed the Easter Rising of 1916 generated considerable support from Irish America (Miller 1985), although the US media were far more critical of the rebellion. When British paratroopers shot and killed 14 unarmed Catholics in 1972, Irish Northern Aid allegedly raised $313,000 within six months of the killings (O'Rourke 1993). Similarly, the donation of funds to Irish Northern Aid increased substantially during the 1980–81 hunger strikes.

Non-financial support has also been considerable. Kevin McKinley and Seamus Moley each received upwards of 20 to 30 letters a day while detained in Florida. One letter was sent from a six-year old child. Another was written by a 16-year old who later convinced her parents to use their house as collateral in order to meet the high bond amount. A 66 year old woman encouraged the Florida defendants to call her collect from jail (Zemen and Rozsa 1990). Matt Morrison had a letter of support provided by the parents of the children whom he coached in St Louis. These forms of support have often served to bolster self-esteem among the individuals affected in the United States. They have eased some of the difficulties associated with incarceration. For deportees and persons facing extradition hearings, letters and telephone calls (even from strangers) provide both confirmation and incentive for the resistance to continue. Moley and McKinley each believed that people become more interested in the cases affecting Irish republicans and also more involved 'when it's on their own doorstep'. Indeed, Tucson, St Louis, Poughkeepsie and areas of South Florida have never been known for their Irish or Irish American communities yet support from within these areas was extensive.

Fundraising and other support, however, have tended to decline or at least taper off, when IRA activity is perceived as damaging.[4] During the 1994 IRA ceasefire, Gerry Adams visited the city of Pittsburgh, Pennsylvania and during the two-day visit he raised $20,000 for the Friends of Sinn Féin. Shortly thereafter, the IRA ended its 17-month ceasefire and some of the people who paid $100 a plate for breakfast with Adams were angered and perplexed. Other reports suggested that fundraising for Sinn Féin had declined substantially after the ceasefire ended (Pope 1996). But in March 1999, in the midst of a reinstated IRA ceasefire, Adams' good standing returned as evidenced by the Pittsburgh-based Duquesne University's announcement of the Gerry Adams' scholarship designed to provide funds for two graduate students from Northern Ireland to study peace studies and conflict resolution through the Center for Social and Public Policy.

Extradition, prosecution and deportation cases that involve Irish republicans in the United States serve to expose the inconsistencies of the British legal system in the north of Ireland. Regarding political trials, Allen (1974, p. 61) noted that the risk for government in political trials is that 'although it may win in the courtroom, it may lose in the larger tribunal'. Joe Doherty, for example, reached groups such as the 'Shamrock Irish' or 'St Patrick's Day Irish' (terms used to describe Irish Americans who have no knowledge of nor interest in Irish history, culture or politics but who proudly claim Irish ancestry on 17 March) whose members had not previously supported Irish freedom. O'Hanlon (1998b, p. 205) noted:

> [Doherty] would have a week in New York proclaimed in his honor while a slice of street outside the forbidding mass of the MCC building, at the junction of Park Row and Pearl Street, would bear the name 'Joseph Doherty Corner.'

Several scholars disseminated information about Doherty's case and discussed allegations of British injustice (see for instance, Baunach 1987; Iversen 1989; Kelly 1992; Scharf 1988). The popular and long-standing national US news show *60 Minutes* featured his case on not one but two occasions. During the trial of Seamus Moley, Kevin McKinley and others, the defence presented historical accounts of eight centuries of British oppression in Ireland and tremendous community sympathy followed. The *Miami Herald* reported: 'Federal agents may refer to them as Irish Republican Army terrorists, but the four have charmed and captured the sympathy of complete strangers who refer to them fondly as "our boys" ' (Rozsa 1990).

Jimmy Smyth received considerable support in his fight against extradition. Most recently an award-winning documentary was released that features his case. Pól Brennan, also facing extradition from the United States, has written several articles that have been published in newspapers in California. Noel Gaynor, who has faced deportation proceedings, and his wife Colleen, have been featured in a number of US newspapers, some mainstream. The Gaynors were also interviewed by CNN. In May 1997 an estimated 22 million viewers were exposed to the C-Span broadcast of the Congressional hearing on the deportees (Hughes 1997b). CBS, a major television broadcasting network in the United States, featured a primetime documentary on three deportation cases in August 1998.[5] News articles have been published in small town papers such as the Jamestown (New York) *Post-Journal*, in urban-based papers such as the *Chicago Tribune*, *Los Angeles Times*, *St Louis Dispatch* and the *San Francisco Chronicle* and in national papers such as *USA Today*. This media exposure draws national attention to the political struggle in the north of Ireland by reaching not only traditional Irish and Irish American enclaves in the United States, but also small towns, villages and rural areas that lack an Irish community. Because these cases have involved Irish nationals residing in the United States, the media there have greater access and journalists have more opportunity to interview the individuals affected. With regards to this media attention, the context is considerably more balanced compared to foreign news of the Irish conflict that has been interpreted by outside journalists. Although the British line might be presented in the article, so too are the Irish nationalist and Irish republican perspectives.

Several of the former prisoners have been invited to speak to both small and large audiences in places like Kansas City, Cleveland, New York, Chicago, Detroit and Richmond, Virginia. As the deportation and extradition cases proceed through the US legal processing, allegations and evidence of human rights violations in Northern Ireland are raised. In the extradition hearings involving Kevin Barry Artt, Pól Brennan and Terence Kirby the issue was raised of collusion between loyalist paramilitaries and members of the police and army. Regardless of whether that argument was accepted by the judiciary and used in its judgment, merely discussing the topic has called attention to an area deemed most sensitive by the British government. Another unintended consequence for the British government is that increased attention to these cases can extend the support base. For example, the Irish Northern Aid chapter in the Poughkeepsie area never existed until Francis Gildernew's arrest. And yet it appears that the British government is willing to risk this adverse attention and expend considerable resources in exchange for a 'successful' extradition or deportation.[6] Why? A British government dismissal of Irish republicans who have sought refuge in the United States would be inconsistent with its Northern Ireland policy. Moreover, there exists the possibility that persons will be returned to Northern Ireland. For each Irish republican extradited or deported, the United States joins its British ally and symbolically rejects the notion of politically-motivated offences in the north of Ireland.

References

Adams, J.M. (1989) 'Reid Seen Drawn to IRA as Radical', *Boston Globe*, 18 July.

Adams, J. (1986) *The Financing of Terror* (Sevenoaks, Kent: New English Library).

Adams, J. (1997) 'Shunning of Sean, the Irish Voice America Won't Hear', *London Times*, 2 March.

Allen, F.A. (1974) *The Crimes of Politics: Political Dimensions of Criminal Justice* (Cambridge, MA: Harvard University).

Alpha 66 (n.d.) *Internet Web Site*. <http://www.alpha66.org>

American Civil Liberties Union (1996) *The Rights of Immigrants* (New York: Author).

American Protestants for Truth About Ireland (1996a) 'Hazardous Plastic Bullets Still Being Used', *Northern Ireland-Human Rights Review*, August.

—— (1996b) 'Shoot-to-Kill is Alleged in O'Neill Death', *Northern Ireland Human Rights Review*, September.

Amnesty International (1988) *United Kingdom-Northern Ireland: Killings by Security Forces and 'Supergrass' Trials* (New York: Author).

—— (1991) *Amnesty International Report: Human Rights Concerns* (New York: Author).

—— (1993) *United Kingdom/Northern Ireland: The Right of Silence* (New York: Author).

—— (1995) *United Kingdom: Summary of Human Rights Concerns* (New York: Author).

—— (1997) *United Kingdom: An Agenda for Human Rights Protection* (New York: Author).

Anderson, B. (1997) 'Loyalists Draw up New RepublicanMurder List', *Irish News*, 24 June.

Anderson, M. (1998) '"The War is Certainly Over" Mowlam Assures Unionists', *Irish News*, 6 August.

Arthur, P. (1991) 'Diasporan Intervention in International Affairs: Irish America as a Case Study', *Diaspora* 1, pp. 143–59.

Asmal, K. (1985) *Shoot to Kill? International Lawyers' Inquiry into the Lethal use of Firearms by the Security Forces in Northern Ireland* (Dublin: Mercier Press).

Associated Press (1997a) Untitled, 27 March.

—— (1997b) 'Bomb Threat Cancels Top British HorseRace', *Los Angeles Times*, 6 April.

Banoff, B.A. and Pyle, C.H. (1984) '"To Surrender Political Offenders": The Political Offense Exception to Extraditionin United States Law', *Journal of International Law and Politics*, 16, pp. 169–210.

Barbash, F. (1997) 'Catholic Anger at Government over Protestant Parade Fuels Violent Disturbances', *Washington Post*, 8 July.

Barlow, M.H.; Barlow, D.E. and Chiricos, T.G. (1995) 'Mobilizing Support for Social Control in a Declining Economy: Exploring Ideologies of Crime within Crime News', *Crime and Delinquency* 41, pp. 191–204.

Bassiouni, M.C. (1974) *International Extradition and World Public Order* (Leyden, Netherlands: A.W. Sijthoff).

—— (1985) *Testimonial Statement*. United States and United Kingdom Supplemental Extradition Treaty: Hearings on Treaty Doc. No.8, Senate Committee on Foreign Relations, 99th Congress, 1st Session (Washington, D.C.: US Government Printing Office).

—— (1996). *International Extradition: United States Law and Practice*, 3rd edition (Dobbs Ferry, NY: Oceana Publications).

Baunach, P.J. (1987) 'The U.S.-U.K. Supplementary Treaty: Justice for Terrorists or Terror for Justice', *Connecticut Journal of International Law*, 2, pp. 463–98.

Belfast Telegraph (1999) 'Ceasefire Has Not the Same Meaning For All', 17 June.

Blake, A. (1991) 'Suspect is Reportedly IRA Member', *Boston Globe*, 12 January.

Blaney, N. (1996) 'Fear of Prisoners Being Used as Pawns', *Irish News*, 12 February.

—— (1998) 'Judge Clears Hamill Murder Case to Proceed', *Irish News*, 13 June.

Borland, J.; King, R.D. and McDermott, K. (1995) 'The Irish in Prison: A Tighter Nick for "the Micks"?' *British Journal of Sociology*, 46, pp. 369–94.

Bowyer Bell, J. (1990) *The Secret Army: The IRA 1916–1979* (Swords: Poolbeg).

Boyer, S. (1996a) 'Government Takes Hard Line on Brian Pearson Deportation', *Irish People*, 30 November.

—— (1996b) 'Will the Real Bill Clinton Please Stand up?', *Irish People*, 2 November.

Brennan, P. (1993) 'A Day of Life in Santa Rita', *Anderson Valley Advertiser*, 25 August.

—— (1994a) 'Starry, Starry Nights', *Anderson Valley Advertiser*, 2 February.

—— (1994b) 'Escape!', *Anderson Valley Advertiser*, 28 September.

—— (1994c) 'Cease Fire!', *Anderson Valley Advertiser*, 7 September.

Broderick, F. (1995) 'A Family's Plea to President Clinton', Letter, *Irish Echo*, 29 November–5 December.

Broderick, F.; Colman, G.; Hegarty, P. and Kilroy, J. (1995) *Where is Liberty? The Prosecution of Irish Republicans in the United States* (Cleveland: Orange Blossom Press).

Builta, J.A. (1995) *Extremist Groups: An International Compilation of Terrorist Organizations, Violent Political Groups, and Issue-Oriented Militant Movements* (Chicago: Office of International Criminal Justice, University of Illinois at Chicago).

Burns, J.F. (1997) 'Northern Ireland: Shattered Lives, Widening Chasm', *Gainesville Sun*, 29 June.

Campbell, B.; McKeown, L., and O'Hagan, F. (1994) *Nor Meekly Serve My Time: The H-Block Struggle 1976–1981* (Belfast: Beyond the Pale).

Carolan, M. (1996) 'IRA Prisoners Plight is "Recipe for Disaster" ' *Irish News*, 16 October.

Carroll, J. (1997) 'Plea to Allow 7 to Stay in US', *Irish Times*, 17 February.

—— (1999) 'Congress May Seek Exclusion of RUC', *Irish Times*, 29 March.

Celmer, M.A. (1987) *Terrorism, U.S. Strategy and Reagan Policies* (Westport, Connecticut: Greenwood Press).

Chermak, S. (1997) 'The Presentation of Drugs in the News Media: The News Sources Involved in the Construction of Social Problems', *Justice Quarterly*, 14, pp. 687–718.

Chicago Tribune (1997) 'Back to the Future in Ulster', editorial, 8 July.

—— (1998) 'Extremists Slay Kin of Sinn Fein Head Adams', 12 January.

Clarity, J.F. (1997) 'Roman Catholics Continue Wave of Violence Across Ulster', *New York Times*, 8 July.

Clarizio, J.B. (1988) 'Report of the Trial of William Joseph Quinn, Central Criminal Court, London'. Unpublished manuscript.

Clark, D.J. (1977) *Irish Blood: Northern Ireland and the American Conscience* (Port Washington, NY: Kennikat Press).

Cockburn, A. (1990) 'An Irishman in Jail Equals a Cuban Out on Bail', *Wall Street Journal*, 26 July.

Committee on the Administration of Justice (1993) *Allegations of Psychological Ill-Treatment of Detainees Held Under Emergency Legislation in Northern Ireland* (Belfast: Author).

—— (1994) *Civil Liberties in Northern Ireland: A Submission to the Clinton Administration* (Belfast: Author).

—— (1998) *Just News*, 13, October.

Connolly, R.E. (1985) *Armalite and Ballot Box: An Irish-American Republican Primer* (Fort Wayne, Indiana: Cuchullain Productions).

Connolly, P. (1997) 'Friends Hurt in Attack', *Belfast Telegraph*, 24 June.

Coogan, T.P. (1993) *De Valera: Long Fellow, Long Shadow* (London: Hutchinson).

—— (1995) *The I.R.A.*, revised edition (London: HarperCollins).

—— (1996) *The Troubles: Ireland's Ordeal 1966–1996 and the Search for Peace* (London: Arrow).

Cornwell, S. (1997) 'No Big Changes in U.S.-U.K. Ties Foreseen', Reuters, 1 May.

Cotton, T. (1994) *The Story of Francis Gildernew*. Working paper.

Cronin, S. (1971*) The Revolutionaries* (Dublin: Republican Publications).

—— (1987) *Washington's Irish Policy 1916–1986* (Dublin: Anvil Books).

Cullen, K. (1997) 'Bolger Hurt IRA Effort, Sources Say,"Whitey" Allegedly Sank Gunrunning Bid', *Boston Globe*, 14 June.

Curtis, L. (1984) *Ireland: The Propaganda War* (London: Pluto Press).

Cusack, J. (1998) 'British Unit Accused of Murder Ties Still at Work', *Irish Times*, 30 March.

Cusack, J. and McDonald, H. (1997) *UVF* (Dublin: Poolbeg).

Deutsch, M.E. and Susler, J. (1991) 'Political Prisoners in the United States: The Hidden Reality', *Humanity and Society*, 15, pp. 350–9.

Dewar, M. (1987) *Weapons and Equipment of Counter-Terrorism* (Poole, Dorset: Arms and Armour Press Limited).

Dietrich, L.J. (1988) 'United States Asylum Policy', in Martin, D.A. (ed.), *The New Asylum Seekers: Refuge Law in the1980s*, pp. 67–72 (Dordrecht, The Netherlands: Kluwer Academic Publishers).

Dillon, M. (1992) *Killer in Clowntown* (London: Arrow Books).

Divine, R.A. (1957) *American Immigration Policy, 1924–1952* (New Haven: Yale University Press).

Dobson, A.P. (1995) *Anglo-American Relations in the Twentieth Century* (London: Routledge).

Doherty, F. (1999) 'FBI are Off Rosemary Case, Dead Loyalist to be Blamed by RUC', *Sunday Business Post*, 25 April.

Domínguez, J.I. (1992) 'Cooperating with the Enemy: U.S. Immigration Policies toward Cuba', in Mitchell, C. (ed.), *Western Hemisphere Immigration and United States Foreign Policy*, pp. 31–88 (University Park, PA: Pennsylvania State University).

Doran, P. (1995) 'Hundreds of Disputed Deaths', *Irish News*, 28 September.

Doran, N. (1998) 'Flanagan Breaks his Silence on SF Ban', *Irish News*, 21 February.

Eilberg, J. and Hamilton, F. (1979) *Northern Ireland: A Role for the United States? Report by Two Members of the Committee on the Judiciary, Factfinding Trip to Northern Ireland, the Irish Republic, and England.* 95th Congress, 2nd session (Washington, D.C.: US Government Printing Office).

Ellison, G. (1997) 'Professionalism in the RUC: An Examination of the Institutional Discourse'. Unpublished PhD (Jordanstown: University of Ulster).

European Committee for the Prevention of Torture (1993) *Site Visit to Interrogation Centre*, July.

Fagen, P.W. (1984) 'Applying for Political Asylum in New York: Law, Policy, and Administrative Practice', *Occasional Paper, No. 41* (New York University: Center for Latin American and Caribbean Studies).

Falk, R. (1988) *Revolutionaries and Functionaries: The Dual Face of Terrorism* (New York: E.P. Dutton).

Farquhar, M. (1999) 'The Real Story of St. Patrick', *Washington Post*, 10 March.

Farrell, M. (1985) *Sheltering the Fugitive? The Extradition of Irish Political Offenders* (Cork: Mercier Press).

Farrow, C. (1997) 'Family of Former IRA Member Fights Deportation', *Post-Journal* (Jamestown, New York), 24 August.

Feeney, B. (1997) 'Loyalist Murders Aren't the Lesser of Two Evils', *Irish News*, 25 June.

Findlay, M. (1985) '"Criminalization" and the Detention of "Political Prisoners" – An Irish Perspective', *Contemporary Crises* 9, pp. 1–17.

Filkins, D. (1991) 'Convicted Irish Activists Allege Entrapment', *Miami Herald*, 6 June.

Fletcher, M. and Rhodes, T. (1996) 'Dole Attacks Clinton for Backing Irish "Terrorist" ' *London Times*, 4 October.

Franklin, H.B. (1997) 'Sketches from Prison (book reviews)', *Washington Post*, 31 August.

Gallagher, T. (1994) *Paddy's Lament: Ireland 1846–1847, Prelude to Hatred* (Swords: Poolbeg).

Gerety, T. (1988) 'Sanctuary: A Comment on the Ironic Relation between Law and Morality', in Martin, D.A. (ed.), *The New Asylum Seekers: Refuge Law in the 1980s*, pp. 159–80 (Dordrecht, The Netherlands: Kluwer Academic Publishers).

Graham, I. (1997) 'Terror Blitz on Republic if Drumcree March Banned', *PA News*, 9 July.

Gray, A. (1999) 'UN Expert Warned Britain of Fear for Killed Lawyer', Reuters, 12 April.

Greenslade, R. (1998) 1st Damien Walsh Memorial Lecture, 4 August, Belfast.

Greer, S. (1990) 'The Supergrass System', in Jennings, A. (ed.), *Justice Under Fire: The Abuse of Civil Liberties in Northern Ireland*, pp. 73–103 (London: Pluto Press).

Guelke, A. (1984) 'The American Nature to the Northern Ireland Conflict', *Irish Studies in International Affairs*, 1, pp. 27–39.

—— (1996) 'The United States, Irish Americans, and the Northern Ireland Peace Process', *International Affairs*, 72, pp. 521–36.

Gunson, P.; Chamberlain, G. and Thompson, A. (1991) *The Dictionary of Contemporary Politics of Central America and the Caribbean* (London: Routledge).

Hailbronner, K. (1988) 'Nonrefoulement and Humanitarian Refugees: Customary International Law or Wishful Legal Thinking', in Martin, D.A. (ed.), *The New Asylum Seekers: Refuge Law in the 1980s*, pp. 123–58 (Dordrecht, The Netherlands: Kluwer Academic Publishers).

Hamm, M.S. (1991)'The Abandoned Ones: A History of the Oakdale and Atlanta Prison Riots', in Barak, G. (ed.), *Crimes by the Capitalist State: An Introduction to State Criminality*, pp. 145–80 (Albany: SUNY Press).

Handlin, O. (1990) 'The Nineteenth Century Immigration', in Tucker, R.W., Keely, C.B. and Wrigley, L. (eds), *Immigration and U.S. Foreign Policy*, pp. 26–39 (Boulder, CO: Westview).

Hartley, S. (1987) *The Irish Question as a Problem in British Foreign Policy, 1914–18* (London: Macmillan).

Hayden, T. (1998) 'Notes of an Irish-American Son',*The Nation*, 18 May.

Herman, E.S. (1982) *The Real Terror Network: Terrorism in Fact and Propaganda* (Montreal: Black Rose Books).

Hickman, M. (1982) 'Crime in the Streets – A Moral Panic: Understanding "Get Tough" Policies in the Criminal Justice System', *Southern Journal of Criminal Justice*, 8, pp. 7–22.

Hoge, W. (1997) 'Britain Convicts 6 of Plot to Black Out London', *New York Times*, 3 July.

Holland, J. (1999) *The American Connection: U.S. Guns, Money, and Influence in Northern Ireland* (Niwot, Colorado: Roberts Rinehart).

Hollywood, B. (1997) 'Dancing in the Dark: Ecstasy, the Dance Culture and Moral Panic in Post Ceasefire Northern Ireland', *Critical Criminology*, 8, pp. 62–7.

Hughes, B. (1997a) 'Did IRA Supply Spaceship for Cult Leaders, Mr. Do?', WBAI Commentary, *Pacifica Radio Free Eireann*, 5 April.
—— (1997b) 'WBAI Commentary', *Pacifica Radio Free Eireann*, 17 May.
Human Rights Watch/Helsinki (1991) *Human Rights in Northern Ireland* (New York: Author).
—— (1993) *Northern Ireland: Continued Abuses by All Sides* (New York: Author).
—— (1994) *Northern Ireland: Continued Abuses by All Sides* (New York: Author).
—— (1997) *To Serve Without Favor: Policing, Human Rights and Accountability* (New York: Author).
Hutchinson, E.P. (1981) *Legislative History of American Immigration Policy, 1798–1965* (Philadelphia: University of Pennsylvania Press).
Irish American Information Service (1998) 'Joe Doherty Released from Maze Prison', 6 November.
Irish Echo (1996) 'U.S. Denies Visas to 3 Ex-Prisoners', 10–16 April.
Irish National Caucus (1993) *Congressional Briefing Paper: The Use of Plastic Bullets in Northern Ireland*, April.
Irish News (1993) 'Irish-Americans Oil the Killing Machine', 18 August.
—— (1997a) 'Brian Pearson Wins Political Asylum', 28 March.
—— (1997b) 'IRA Truce on Clinton Agenda', 29 May.
—— (1997c) 'IRA Planned Huge Hoax to Cause London Chaos', 5 June.
—— (1998a) 'Governments Set out Case for Sinn Féin's Expulsion', 21 February.
—— (1998b) 'Americans Haven't a Clue About', Letter to the editor, 27 March.
Irish People (1996) 'Mixey Martin Repatriated', 10 February.
—— (1997) 'Britain Leading in Human Rights Violations', 18 January.
Iversen, G.C. (1989) 'Just Say No! United States Options to Extradition to the North of Ireland's Diplock Court System', *Loyola of Los Angeles International and Comparative Law Journal,* 12, pp. 249–80.
Jennings, A. (1990) 'Shoot-to-Kill: The Final Courts of Justice', in Jennings, A. (ed.), *Justice Under Fire: The Abuse of Civil Liberties in Northern Ireland*, pp. 104–30 (London: Pluto Press).
Johnson, P. (1980) *Ireland: A Concise History from the Twelfth Century to the Present Day* (Chicago: Academy Chicago Publishers).

Kee, R. (1972) *The Bold Fenian Men*, Green Flag, Vol. II (London: Penguin Books).

Kelly, J.T. (1992) 'The Empire Strikes Back: The Taking of Joe Doherty', *Fordham Law Review*, LXI, pp. 317–99.

Keneally, T. (1998) *The Great Shame: A Story of the Irish in the Old World and the New* (London: BCA).

Kennedy, E. (1998) *Northern Ireland – A View from America*, Tip O'Neill Memorial Lecture, University of Ulster, Magee College, Derry, 9 January.

Kincheloe, P.J. (1999) 'Two Visions of Fairyland: Ireland and the Monumental Discourse of the Nineteenth-Century American Tourist', *Irish Studies Review*, 7, pp. 41–52.

Kingston, S. (1995) 'Terrorism, the Media, and the Northern Ireland Conflict', *Studies in Conflict and Terrorism*, 18, pp. 203–31.

Kittrie, N.N. and Wedlock, E.D., (eds) (1986) *The Tree of Liberty: A Documentary History of Rebellion and Political Crime in America* (Baltimore: Johns Hopkins University Press).

Knox, C. (1999) 'Who are the Victims?', *Fortnight*, May, pp. 11–12.

Lafree, G.D. (1989) *Rape and Criminal Justice: The Social Construction of Sexual Assault* (Belmont, California: Wadsworth).

Lawyers Committee for Human Rights (1996a) *1995 Critique – Introduction* (New York: Author).

—— (1996b) *At the Crossroads: Human Rights and theNorthern Ireland Peace Process* (New York: Author).

Lent, J.A. (1977) 'Foreign News in American Media', *Journal of Communication*, 27, pp. 46–51.

Lewis, A. (1999) 'Abroad at Home: A Heedless Court', *New York Times*, 13 March.

Loftus, J. and McIntyre, E. (1989) *Valhalla's Wake: The IRA, MI6, and the Assassination of a Young American* (New York: Atlantic Monthly Press).

London Times (1986) 'Reciprocity in Washington' (editorial), 22 April.

—— (1997) 'Green at the Edges' (editorial), 13 February.

Los Angeles Times (1997) 'Once Again, IRA Violence has Closed the Door to Negotiations', 18 June.

—— (1998) 'Ulster Must Escape its History', 8 July.

Mac an Bhaird, C. (1996) 'Dole Backs "United Ireland" ', *Irish People*, 21 September.

—— (1997a) 'The Cheeky Wheel Gets the Grease', *Irish People*, 4 February.

—— (1997b) 'H-Block Three Squeezed: Brennan in Hole; Artt moved to Oakland', *Irish People*, 4 October.

—— (1997c) 'Glamor, Glitz Overshadow Death in North of Ireland', *Irish People*, 21 July.

MacLeod, A. (1998) 'Britain Links its Support of US Against Iraq to Help on Belfast', *Christian Science Monitor*, 2 February.

MacUileagóid, M. (1996) *From Fetters to Freedom: The Inside Story of Irish Jailbreaks* (Belfast: SASTA).

Maloney, E. (1998) 'UN to Seek Inquiry into Finucane Killing', *Sunday Tribune*, 29 March.

Maranz, S. (1984) *Immigration: Asylum Issues*, Issue Brief Number IB83119, 13 June (Washington, D.C.: Congressional Research Service, Library of Congress).

Marshall, F. (1996) 'Maze Escapee McNally Living Just Across Irish Border', *PA News*, October 19.

Martin-Clarke, N. (1998) 'Committee Author Stands Firm', *Irish Voice*, 23 December.

McAleer, P. (1997a) 'America Halts IRA Men's Deportation', *Irish News*, 10 September.

—— (1997b) 'America Drops IRA from Blacklist', *Irish News*, 9 October.

McCartan, D. and Purdy, M. (1997) 'London Sidesteps Deportation Row – Decision an Issue for US Authorities', *Belfast Telegraph*, 10 September.

McClellan, B. (1994) 'Couple is Hoping Peace Goes from N. Ireland to U. City', *St. Louis Dispatch*, 2 September.

—— (1997) 'Man Won Battle, but His Wife Was the True Warrior', *St. Louis Dispatch*, 12 September.

McCluskey, C. (1989) *Up off Their Knees: A Commentary on the Civil Rights Movement in Northern Ireland* (Galway: Conn McCluskey and Associates).

McCoy, K. (1998) 'Doherty May Gain Freedom', *New York Daily News*, 15 April.

McGeough, G. (1996) *The Ambush and Other Stories: A Selection of Prison Writings* (N.L.: Jay Street Publishers).

McGurk, T. (1999) 'Northern Judges and Northern Justice', *Sunday Business Post*, 28 March.

McKinney, J. (1997) 'The News Media Bury Another "Cease-fire" Victim', *Philadelphia Inquirer*, 16 May.

McKinney, S. (1999) 'RUC Hit with New Finucane Allegation: Police "Failed to Warn Solicitor"', *Irish News*, 10 March.

McKittrick, D. (1999) 'British Security Services "Colluded with Loyalists" in Six Counties', *Independent*, 3 May.

McManus, Fr. S. (1993) *The MacBride Principles: Genesis and History to Date* (Washington, D.C.: Irish National Caucus).

McPhilemy, S. (1998) *The Committee: Political Assassination in Northern Ireland* (Niwot, Colorado: Roberts Rinehart).

Meissner, D. (1988) 'Reflections on the Refugee Act of 1980', in Martin, D.A. (ed.), *The New Asylum Seekers: Refuge Law in the 1980s*, pp. 57–66 (Dordrecht, The Netherlands: Kluwer Academic Publishers).

Metress, S.P. (1995) *Outlines in Irish History: Eight Hundred Years of Struggle* (Detroit: Connolly Books).

Millar, F. (1997) 'O'Callaghan to Challenge Peace Process on US Tour', *Irish Times*, 19 February.

Miller, D. (1994) *Don't Mention the War: Northern Ireland, Propaganda and the Media* (London: Pluto Press).

Miller, K.A. (1985) *Emigrants and Exiles: Ireland and the Irish Exodus to North America* (New York: Oxford University Press).

Miller, K. and Wagner, P. (1994) *Out of Ireland: The Story of Irish Emigration to America* (Washington, D.C.: Elliott and Clark).

Mitchell, C. (1992) 'Introduction: Immigration and U.S. Foreign Policy toward the Caribbean, Central America, and Mexico', in Mitchell, C. (ed.), *Western Hemisphere Immigration and United States Foreign Policy*, pp. 1–30 (University Park, PA: Pennsylvania State University).

Moloney, E. (1991) 'Closing Down the Airwaves: The Story of the Broadcasting Ban', in Rolston, B. (ed.), *The Media and Northern Ireland: Covering the Troubles*, pp. 8–50 (London: Macmillan).

Montalbano, W.D. (1997a) 'Hundreds in N. Ireland Mourn Police Slain by IRA', *Los Angeles Times*, 18 June.

—— (1997b) 'Terrorists Resume Havoc in Britain', *Los Angeles Times*, 19 April.

—— (1997c) 'IRA Code Words Spell Real Threat', *Los Angeles Times*, 19 April.

—— (1998) 'On His First Trip to Northern Ireland, a Kennedy Symbolizes Hope', *Los Angeles Times*, 11 January.

Morrison, M. (1996) Public Lecture, Fort Lauderdale, Florida, February.

Mulcahy, A. (1995) 'Claims-Making and the Construction of Legitimacy: Press Coverage of the 1981 Northern Irish Hunger Strike', *Social Problems*, 42, pp. 449–67.

Murphy, P. (1998) 'Blair Praises Clinton's "Solid" Support over Ulster', *PA News*, 3 February.

Murray, R. (1998) *State Violence in Northern Ireland 1969–1997* (Dublin: Mercier).

Nadelmann, E.A. (1993) 'The Evolution of United States Involvement in the International Rendition of Fugitive Criminals', *New York University Journal of International Law and Politics*, 25, pp. 813–85.

Naughton, M. (1996) 'Pete the Para Paid Back', *An Phoblacht/Republican News*, 14 November.

New York Times (1997a) 'Tony Blair's Irish Peace Plan', 27 June.

—— (1997b) 'Half-Measures on British Freedoms', 17 November.

Northern Ireland Office (1989) *Press Release*, L 56/89.

Norton-Taylor, R. (1997) 'Spies Targeted Irish Groups in the US', *Irish Times*, 23 October.

O'Brien, B. (1995) *The Long War: the IRA and Sinn Féin from Armed Struggle to Peace Talks* (Dublin: O'Brien Press).

Ó Broin, L. (1971) *Fenian Fever: An Anglo-American Dilemma* (London: Chatto and Windus).

O'Carroll, C. (1997) 'Hunt Ongoing for IRA Weapon', *Irish News*, 14 April.

O'Cathaoir, B. (1990) *John Blake Dillon, Young Irelander* (Blackrock: Irish Academic Press).

O'Clery, C. (1995) 'Special Relationship Only a Memory as Unanswered Call Gives a Ringing Message', *Irish Times*, 18 March.

—— (1996a) *The Greening of the White House* (Dublin: Macmillan).

—— (1996b) 'US Agrees to Transfer of Irish Prisoner to Dublin', *Irish Times*, 30 January.

O'Coileain, L. (1996) 'British Tendered Forged Documents', *An Phoblacht/Republican News*, 12 December.

O'Dowd, N. (1998) 'Clinton's Debt to Irish-Americans', *Sunday Times*, 18 January.

O'Dwyer, Paul (1979) *Counsel for the Defense: The Autobiography of Paul O'Dwyer* (New York: Simon and Schuster).

Office of the Press Secretary (1997a) *White House Press Briefing*, 15 July.

—— (1997b) *White House Press Briefing*, 3 July.

Ogden, C. (1990) *Maggie: The Portrait of a Woman in Power* (New York: Simon and Schuster).

O'Grady, J. (1996) 'An Irish Policy Born in the U.S.A.', *Foreign Affairs*, May/June, pp. 2–7.

O'Grady, J.P. (1976) *Irish-Americans and Anglo-American Relations, 1880–1888* (New York: Arno Press).

O'Hanlon, R. (1996a) 'McMullen is Flown Back to Britain', *Irish Echo*, 3–9 April.

—— (1996b) 'Clinton Bids to Quell Storm Over MacBride', *Irish News*, 28 August.

—— (1997a) 'New Twist in Pearson IRA Deportation', *Irish News*, 5 March.

—— (1997b) 'Sinn Fein's US Funds Top $2.3m Since 1995', *Sunday Business Post*, 28 December.

—— (1997c) 'Why Clinton Fought Tough over Change to Terror List', 10 October.

—— (1998a) 'Irish-American Nerves Crave a Dose of Unity', *Irish News*, 17 November.

—— (1998b) *The New Irish Americans* (Niwot, Colorado: Roberts Rinehart).

O'Neill, J. (1995a) 'Facing Jail, Smyth Appeals to Clinton', *Irish Echo*, August 9–15.

—— (1995b) 'Smyth Slams San Francisco Mayor over Stance on Prisoners', *Irish Echo*, 26 July–1 August.

O'Rourke, H.E. (1993) 'The Fenian Tradition: Its Influence on Support for Irish Revolutionary Groups by Irish-Americans', Paper presented at the Annual Meetings of the American Society of Criminology, Phoenix, Arizona, November.

Parker, T. (1994) *May the Lord in His Mercy be Kind to Belfast* (New York: Henry Holt).

—— (1995) *The Violence of Our Lives* (New York: Henry Holt).

Pat Finucane Centre (1997) *Ronnie Flanagan: A Fact File on the RUC Chief Constable* (Derry: Author).

Pope, K. (1996) 'IRA's Bombing Campaign is Damaging U.S. Financial Support for Sinn Féin', *Wall Street Journal*, 1 July.

Prebensen, D. (1997) 'Scotland Yard Targets Deportee Families', *Irish People*, 15 February.

Preston, W. (1963) *Aliens and Dissenters: Federal Suppression of Radicals, 1903–1933* (Cambridge, Massachusetts: Harvard University Press).

Ridgeway, J. and Farrelly, P. (1994) 'The Belfast Connection', *Village Voice*, 8 February, pp. 29–36.

Riley, J. (1986) 'Is U.S. Playing Politics with Extradition?' *National Law Journal*, 16 June, pp. 3, 8.

RM Distribution (1999) 'History: General Amnesty 1917', *Irish News Round-Up*, 16 June.

Roebuck, W. (1994) 'Extradition-Denial of Asylum-Withholding Deportation-Different Tactics by the Attorney General to Deliver Provisional Irish Republican Army Members to the British: Doherty v. United States, 908 F.2d 1108 (2d Cir. 1990)' *Georgia Journal of International and Comparative Law*, 20, pp. 665–83.

Rosenfeld, S.S. (1997) 'Sinn Féin, Terrorism and Us', *Washington Post*, 5 September.

Royal Ulster Constabulary (1995) *Chief Constable's Annual Report* (Belfast: HMSO).

Rozsa, L. (1990) 'Accused Terrorists Intrigue Locals', *Miami Herald*, 21 January.

Rozsa, Lori and Zeman, D. (1990) '3 Guilty of Weapons Conspiracy – U.S. Role Blasted in Irishmen's Case', *Miami Herald*, 12 December.

RTE (1999) 'Use of Plastic Bullets in NI to Continue', *RTE Briefs*, 1 February.

Ryan, M. (1994) *War and Peace in Ireland: Britain and the IRA in the New World Order* (London: Pluto Press).

Said, E.W. (1997) *Covering Islam: How the Media and the Experts Determine How we See the Rest of the World* (London: Vintage).

Scally, D. (1998) 'Deportees Blast CBS Documentary', *Irish Voice Online*, 24 August.

Scharf, M.P. (1988) 'Foreign Courts on Trial: Why U.S. Courts Should Avoid Applying the Inquiry Provision of the Supplementary U.S.-U.K. Extradition Treaty', *Stanford Journal of International Law*, 25, pp. 257–88.

Scherr, E.F. (1997) 'Backgrounder on U.S. Report on Human Rights', Internet Web Site, http://www.usia.gov/topical/rights/hrpage/backgerg.htm.

Schoultz, L. (1992) 'Central America and the Politicization of U.S. Immigration Policy', in Mitchell, C. (ed.), *Western Hemisphere Immigration and United States Foreign Policy*, pp. 157–219 (University Park, PA: Pennsylvania State University).

Schrecker, E. (1996–1997) 'Immigration and Internal Security: Political Deportations during the McCarthy Era', *Science and Society* 60, pp. 393–426.

Schweid, B. (1997) 'Clinton', *Associated Press*, 29 May.

Shannon, C.B. (1993) 'The Kennedys, Ireland and Irish America: A Healthy Intersection,' *The Irish Review*, Autumn, pp. 10–14.

Shearer, I.A. (1971) *Extradition in International Law* (Manchester: University of Manchester Press).

Sillard, P.A. (1908) *Life of John Mitchel* (Dublin: J. Duffy).

Simpson, M. (1997a) 'Mitchell Takes on Tobacco Lobbyist Role', *Belfast Telegraph*, 9 June.

—— (1997b) 'Mitchell Shows Staying Powers at Stormont', *Belfast Telegraph*, 10 June.

Smith, B.L. (1993) 'Punishing Political Offenders: An Analysis of Sentences Imposed on "Officially Designated Terrorists"', paper presented at the Annual Meetings of the American Society of Criminology, Phoenix, Arizona, November.

Smith, B.L. and Damphouse, K.R. (1996) 'Punishing Political Offenders: The Effect of Political Motive on Federal Sentencing Decisions', *Criminology*, 34, pp. 289–321.

Smith, R.J. (1997) '18 Groups Penalized for Aiding Terrorists', *Washington Post*, 9 October.

Smith, M.L.R. (1997) *Fighting for Ireland? The Military Strategy of the Irish Republican Movement* (London: Routledge).

Smith, S.J. (1984) 'Crime in the News', *British Journal of Criminology*, 24, pp. 289–95.

Southern Poverty Law Center (1995) *Klanwatch: Intelligence Report,* March (Montgomery, Alabama: Author).

Spohn, C. (1994) 'Crime and the Social Control of Blacks: Offender/Victim Race and the Sentencing of Violent Offenders', in Bridges, G.S. and Myers, M.M. (eds), *Inequality, Crime and Social Control* (Boulder, Colorado: Westview).

Stohl, M. (1988) 'National Interests and State Terrorism in International Affairs', in *The Politics of Terrorism*, 3rd edition, Stohl, M. (ed.), pp. 273–92 (New York: Marcel Dekker).

Stout, K. and Dello Buono, R.A. (1991) 'Political Prisoners as an Emergent Contradiction of State Repression: An Introductory Essay', *Humanity and Society*, 15, pp. 338–49.

Susler, J. (1995) 'Nelson Mandela is Alive and Well in Prison in the United States', *Humanity and Society*, 19, pp. 75–84.

Tansill, C.C. (1957) *America and the Fight for Irish Freedom, 1866–1922* (New York: Devin-Adair).

Taylor, P. (1996) 'The Semantics of Political Violence', in Rolston, B. and Miller, D. (eds), *War and Words: The Northern Ireland Media Reader*, pp. 329–39 (Belfast: Beyond the Pale Publications).

—— (1997) *Provos: The IRA and Sinn Féin* (London: Bloomsbury).

Thomas, J. (1991) 'Toeing the Line: Why the American Press Fails', in Rolston, B. (ed.), *The Media and Northern Ireland: Covering the Troubles*, pp. 122–35 (London: Macmillan).

Tomlinson, M. (1998) 'Walking Backwards into the Sunset: British Policy and the Insecurity of Northern Ireland', in Miller, D. (ed.), *Rethinking Northern Ireland: Culture, Ideology and Colonialism* (London: Longman).

Trainor, L. (1998) 'Murder was over Money Claim', *Irish News*, 12 February.

Tugwell, M. (1981) 'Politics and Propaganda of the Provisional IRA', *Terrorism: An International Journal*, 5, pp. 13–40.

Turner, J. (1998) 'British Told Investigate Murder of Solicitor', *Irish News*, 1 April.

—— (1999) '150 Names on Hit-List Admits RUC' *Irish News*, 19 May.

United Campaign Against Plastic Bullets (1996) 'A Report on the Misuse of the Baton Round in the North of Ireland', Submission to the Mitchell Commission on Arms Decommissioning, Belfast.

United Nations Committee Against Torture (1995) *Committee Finding*. November.

United Nations General Assembly (1973) *Basic Principles of the Legal Status of the Combatants Struggling against Colonial and Alien Domination and Racist Régimes*, 12 December.

United Nations Human Rights Commission (1995) *Committee Finding*, July.

—— (1998) *Report by Special Rapporteur on the Independence of Judges and Lawyers*, April.

United States Arms Control and Disarmament Agency (1998) 'World Military Expenditures and Arms Transfers', Internet Web Site, http://www.acda.gov/factshee/conwpn/wmeatsfs.htm.

United States Bureau of Census (1996) *Exports Commodity Report, Arms and Ammunition, Parts and Accessories thereof Exported to the United Kingdom* (Washington, D.C.: Author).

United States Code (n.d.) 8 USC sec. 1158.

United States Department of State (1995) *US Exports: Foreign Policy Controls, Fact File*. Washington, D.C.: United States Department of State, Bureau of Public Affairs.

—— (1996) *Country Reports on Human Rights Practices: United Kingdom/Northern Ireland, 1995*, Website: http://www.state.gov/www/global/human_rights/hrp_reports_mainhp.html

—— (1997a) *Country Reports on Human Rights Practices: United Kingdom/Northern Ireland, 1996*, Website: http://www.state.gov/www/global/human_rights/1996_hrp_report/unitedki.html

—— (1997b) *Designation of Foreign Terrorist Organizations, Fact Sheet*, Website: http://www.state.gov/www/global/terrorism/fs_terrorist_orgs.html

—— (1997c) *Patterns of Global Terrorism, 1997: Europe and Eurasia Overview, United Kingdom*, Website: http://www.state.gov/www/global/terrorism/1997report/eurasia.html

United States Senate (1984) 'Issues Relating to the Deportation of Michael O'Rourke', *Hearings before the Subcommittee on the Constitution of the Committee on the Judiciary*, 18 June, 30 July.

Vargo, T.Y. (1998) 'A LOOK AT...The Irish, Here and There: For Irish Americans, Peace Means Change', *Washington Post*, 19 July.

Walker, S.; Spohn, C. and DeLone, M. (1996) *The Color of Justice: Race, Ethnicity and Crime in America* (Belmont, California: Wadsworth).

Ward, A.J. (1968) 'America and the Irish Problem', *Irish Historical Studies*, 16 pp. 64–90.

Ward, K. (1984) 'Ulster Terrorism: The US Network News coverage of Northern Ireland 1968–1979', in Alexander, Y. and O'Day, A. (eds), *Terrorism in Ireland*, pp. 201–12 (London: Croom Helm).

Washington Post (1997) 'A Welcome to the IRA', 3 September.

Weiss, R.S. (1994) *Learning from Strangers: The Art and Method of Qualitative Interview Studies* (New York: Free Press).

White, R.W. (1993) 'On Measuring Political Violence: Northern Ireland, 1969 to 1980', *American Sociological Review*, 58, pp. 575–85.

Willing, R. (1997) 'Ruling Gives Ex-IRA Bomber Hope of American Dream', *USA Today*, 14 April.

Wilson, A.J. (1994) 'The Conflict between Noraid and the Friends of Irish Freedom: Trends in Modern Irish-American Republicanism, 1980–1992', *The Irish Review*, Spring, pp. 40–50.

—— (1995) *Irish America and the Ulster Conflict, 1968–1995* (Belfast: Blackstaff Press).

Woodham-Smith, Cecil (1962) *The Great Hunger: Ireland 1845–1849* (New York: Old Town Books).

Wright, S. (1978) 'New Police Technologies: An Exploration of the Social Implications and Unforeseen Impacts of Some Recent Developments', *Journal of Peace Research*, 25, pp. 305–22.

Zemen, D. and Rozsa, L. (1990) 'Suspect in IRA Terrorism, Case Apt to Make Bail', *Miami Herald*, 22 July.

Zolberg, A.R. (1990) 'The Roots of U.S. Refugee Policy', in Tucker, R.A.; Keely, C.B. and Wrigley, L. (eds), *Immigration and U.S. Foreign Policy*, pp. 99–120 (Boulder, CO: Westview).

Case Cited

In the matter of James Smyth, 863 F. Supp. 1137 (1994)
Quinn v. *Robinson*, 783 F. 2d 776 (9th Cir. 1986)

Statutes Cited

8 US Code 1158, Aliens and Nationality

Appendices

Research Context and Background

The material in this book is drawn from several sources, including mainstream and specialised newspapers, published documents from Irish and Irish American support groups, historical records, academic and mainstream articles and books and congressional testimony. Additional data were collected through interviews with Irish republicans in the United States who have been convicted in US courts, or who have faced extradition or deportation hearings in the United States.[1] Discussions were also held with two Irish nationals in the United States who, unbeknown to the INS, had been imprisoned previously in the north of Ireland and had either entered the United States under a false name or had overextended a visa expiration date. Both men had been released from a British prison in the north of Ireland, after serving several years for politically-motivated offences. Their identities were not known to me. Finally, interviews and discussions were conducted with US residents or citizens who were active in defence groups (organised to assist Irish political prisoners in the United States) or in other US groups that supported the Irish republican movement.

The small group of interviewees upon which selected findings were based are not intended to represent the views of the Irish republican movement in Ireland, the United States or elsewhere. Rather, they are based on responses from a small number of people without the benefit of random sampling. Some of the interview data are rich in detail but pen and paper were rarely used (see below) and tape recorders were not a viable option, so that the number of quotations was limited. The data do provide, however, a series of frameworks for describing issues that pertain to people's experiences with the US legal and immigration systems as they apply to prosecution, extradition and deportation. Discussions with republican supporters helped to identify myths associated with Irish America, Irish Northern Aid and other sources of support.

Procedures for Interviews and Settings

Persons held in US prisons and jails were the easiest group to identify and locate. Prisoners' addresses were printed in several Irish and Irish-American newspapers or were available from support groups. Other individuals were located through support groups or defence committees and various documents.

Although Irish republicans incarcerated in the United States were easy to locate, interviews conducted in jails and prisons were at times problematic. In *Violence of Our Lives*, Tony Parker (1995, p. xvii) commented on the 'arcane and bureaucratic' structure to which one must adhere in order to gain research access to federal prisoners in the United States. Had I read his warning before I had posted the letters of introduction, I might have changed my mind. I was accustomed to the procedures used in state prisons, having conducted research in those sites on a few occasions. Never would I have anticipated the amount of time and effort involved in trying to organise interviews within the federal prison system.

For three interviews, I was first asked by the Bureau of Prisons (BOP) to submit a lengthy research proposal (approximately 15 typed pages) that described my study. Copies of the proposal were sent to the prison warden and to the BOP central office in Washington, D.C. In the proposal I requested two-hour interviews with three prisoners. I noted that I would be willing to make separate trips or that group interviews could be conducted if that procedure would relieve the burden to correctional officers (recognising, however, that group interviews at times are not as informative).

Several weeks later I received notice that the warden of the prison had refused my request for interviews. He reasoned that because prisoner riots had occurred several months before, my interviews might disrupt the security of the prison. I could still arrange 'regular visits' with the prisoners but these meetings would have to be held without the benefit of pen and paper. I appealed the warden's decision to the BOP and under the Freedom of Information Act I requested copies of all research proposals that had been approved by the warden during the past five years. I also informed the warden that since journalists (as opposed to researchers) were permitted to interview prisoners, I assumed that it would be permissible to send a journalist in my place. I then contacted a Florida state senator and asked him for assistance. I received a fax from the BOP within weeks after I filed the appeal; the warden had reconsidered and I was permitted to interview with pen and paper.

The warden's approval allowed me to take notes during the interviews with two prisoners (the permission process took several months during which time a third prisoner had been released). Prison staff, however, did not appear to be overjoyed about the warden's decision. A female member of the prison administrative staff sat quietly about 75 feet from where I was interviewing during the entire session. At times, questions and responses were voiced in quiet tones so that she could not overhear our discussion. She promptly ended the interview at the scheduled time and escorted me to the prison gates without further comment.

I had arranged for another interview with a prisoner in a different facility for which the documentation had been completed for visitation (that is, my name had to be added to the prisoner's list of accepted visitors and approved by prison staff). During written correspondence I had informed the staff about the purpose of my visit. I made flight arrangements and had reserved a car and hotel room. The day before the interview I contacted the prison in order to obtain directions from the airport at which time I was told that an interview was not permitted. A 'regular visit' was allowed but that type of visit would not permit me to use pen and paper during our meeting. The decision was subject to internal appeal by the warden and I complied with his instructions by sending a fax on university stationery that explained my need for pen and paper. As I boarded the airline the next day, I had no idea whether I would be permitted to use the writing tools during the interview (in the end the pen and paper remained in the car).

Prison staff also informed me that if they perceived that I was conducting an interview rather than a 'regular visit' the meeting would be terminated and I would be asked to leave. After examining my surroundings in the visitation area I do not know how prison officials would ever have known that I had carried out an interview. Why prison officials cared is another question; in this instance the prisoner was scheduled to be released within a few months after the interview was to take place.

On those occasions when pen and paper were not permitted during prison visits, I followed the suggestions of other researchers (see for example, Weiss 1994, p. 55) and took notes in quiet settings (for example, rental cars, hotel rooms) as soon as possible after leaving the prison. Some information, no doubt, was lost as a result of this procedure but at times it was the only viable option.

In a jail setting the correctional officers did not examine any materials in my possession and I entered the visitation area with pen and paper exposed. In this setting I was permitted to take notes during the interview although a glass panel separated us. At times the noise level in the jail made it difficult for us to hear one another but no other visits were occurring at the time so distractions were minimal. It was the only site at which correctional officers appeared to assist me. For instance, initially I was permitted a two-hour interview but officers allowed us to extend the visit by at least one hour when they became aware of the distance that I had travelled.[2]

Interviews were generally conducted during regular visitation hours and amidst several other visits. Chairs were placed side-by-side and in fixed positions so that persons could not face each other during conversation. The disadvantage of this setting was that at times it was difficult to concentrate in the midst of other visits and activities. However, these types of visits were also advantageous in that they lasted for several hours so that more topics could be discussed.

Interviews with persons who have faced deportation hearings took place in public settings, often in restaurants or quiet pubs. Sometimes friends or spouses accompanied the interviewee. After the initial interview, we often maintained contact (although infrequently) which allowed for an open door should I have subsequent questions.

Interviews and discussions with persons who were involved in one of several support groups were conducted in various public places. A few contacts helped to arrange meetings with two former political prisoners from the north of Ireland, who at the time were residing in the United States, without the knowledge of the INS.

I provided all funding for this study, including funds for several out-of-state trips to conduct the interviews.[3] At times, travel expenditures were costly, however, the advantages of self-funding far outweighed the expenses. For instance, self-funding provided me with the luxury of not having to comply with an agenda – spoken or otherwise – of the funding institution. I developed my own set of questions and let the interview flow from there.

Table 1 Murder victims of Loyalist violence, 1996 to 1999, during alleged loyalist ceasefire

Date	Victim	Comments
July 1996	Michael McGoldrick, Catholic	Murdered by the Loyalist Volunteer Force.
March 1997	John Slane, Catholic	Murdered in his home in West Belfast.
May 1997	Robert Hamill, Catholic	Beaten to death by a 30-strong loyalist mob in Portadown.
May 1997	Sean Brown, Catholic	Abducted in Bellaghy; body found in Randalstown.
June 1997	Gregory Taylor, off-duty RUC officer	Beaten to death by a loyalist mob outside a pub in Ballymoney. Eight males accused of the crime. One granted bail in March 1998.
July 1997	Bernadette Martin, Catholic	Murdered by the LVF in Aghalee while she slept in the home of her Protestant boyfriend's family. One convicted of murder.
July 1997	James Morgan, 16-year-old Catholic	The killers carved the initials of the loyalist organisation on Morgan's chest. Killers tried to hide the body under piles of animal carcasses. Mutilated body found in Clough. LVF member Norman Coopey was charged and convicted of the murder.
October 1997	Glen Greer, Protestant	It was believed that loyalist paramilitaries were responsible for the car bomb attack.
December 1997	Gerry Devlin, Catholic	Member of St Edna's Gaelic Athletic Association. Murdered by loyalists in Glengormley. More than a dozen members of the club had been attacked in previous years.

Date	Name	Notes
December 1997	Seamus Dillon, Catholic	Murdered by the LVF in Dungannon while working as a doorman at a hotel club. At the time, the club was full of teenagers attending a Christmas disco.
December 1997	Eddie Treanor, Catholic	Murdered during a gun attack.
January 1998	Larry Brennan, Catholic	
January 1998	Ben Hughes	
January 1998	Terry Enright	Murdered by the LVF.
January 1998	John McGolgan, Catholic	
January 1998	Liam Conway, Catholic	Floral tributes at the scene of the murder were scattered and burned.
January 1998	Fergal McCusker	Murdered by the LVF.
March 1998	Philip Allen, Protestant and Damien Trainor, Catholic	Murdered by the LVF.
April 1998	Adrian Lamph, Catholic	Murdered by the LVF.
April 1998	Ciaran Heffron, Catholic	Murdered.
July 1998	Richard Mark and Jason Quinn, Catholic children	Died after loyalists burned their home.
October 1998	Brian Service, Catholic	Red Hand Defenders.
March 1999	Rosemary Nelson, Human rights lawyer	Clients included the family of Robert Hamill (above).

Notes

Introduction

1. This description is limited in that it fails to include native Americans, many of whom were victims of genocide, and also excludes most persons of African descent who were forced to emigrate and were subsequently enslaved.
2. In the United States, political asylum is granted for persons who show past persecution or show a 'well-founded fear of persecution' (8 United States Code 1158) on account of their race, nationality, religion, or political opinion.
3. Long Kesh prison was officially renamed Her Majesty's Prison-Maze in the 1970s. Several persons, however, continue to refer to the prison by its former name.
4. Internet sources continue to expand people's knowledge about the Irish conflict. US-based web sites include several sources for information on Irish political prisoners in the United States. News groups and discussion lists also serve to distribute information and contribute to the knowledge base of the conflict.

Chapter 1

1. The Young Ireland movement began in 1846 and was composed of Catholics and Protestants alike. The movement's leaders distributed various literature that justified and encouraged armed struggle against British rule in Ireland. The 1848 rising was not successful in this respect. Some analysts suggest that the Movement was unsuccessful in its military strategy because of lack of spirit among the Irish people; hunger, disease and death from these hardships being the more salient issues (Woodham-Smith 1962).
2. Thomas Francis Meagher was appointed Governor of Montana but drowned in 1867 before his service began (Woodham-Smith 1962).
3. Subsequently called the Irish Republican Brotherhood.

4. Clan na Gael was founded in 1867 and within six years had established 87 chapters in the United States (O'Rourke 1993).
5. Later, Clan na Gael donated $5,000 towards Roger Casement's defence (in Hartley 1987, p. 82).
6. Thomas Clarke, however, was a US citizen through naturalisation. That status apparently did not grant him leniency as he was executed in 1916 for his role in the Easter Rising.
7. In reviewing the de Valera Papers, Coogan (1993) noted, however, that de Valera dismissed the notion that his American affiliation saved his life.
8. Recognising that for some people the word 'famine' is an inappropriate term used to describe the Great Hunger, the word is used here only as a term of reference which most people understand.
9. Woodrow Wilson was descended from Scottish/English (Protestant) planters who resided near Strabane, County Tyrone. During his presidential term, Protestant paramilitaries were organising in the north of Ireland in an effort to resist Home Rule.
10. His sister, Jean Kennedy Smith, former Ambassador to Ireland (south), was considerably more outspoken and proactive with regards to the north (see Chapter 6).
11. On 30 January 1972, 13 unarmed civil rights demonstrators were killed by members of the first Parachute Regiment of the British Army in Derry, north of Ireland. Another died later from injuries.
12. In October 1996 I spoke with staff of the Office of Trade Controls, US Department of State. I inquired about the sales of weaponry for use by the RUC and asked specifically about the duration of the transactions and when precisely they had been prohibited. The staff member stated, 'Our records don't go back that far.'

Chapter 2

1. For example, in 1907 the US Senate appointed the Dillingham Commission whose purpose was to examine immigration patterns to the United States. The Commission concluded that post-1880 immigrants to the United States came largely from eastern and southern Europe and recommended that literacy tests be implemented as a method of halting the flow of immigrants from these regions.

2. The Refugee Act of 1980 repealed the limitations which had previously favoured refugees from communist countries and from the Middle East.

3. Prosecutions commenced before this time. See Chapter 4.

4. Until the detention of Joseph Doherty, that is. See Chapter 3.

5. Diplock courts were implemented in 1973 and were designed to hear cases involving defendants charged with 'scheduled offences' (for example, murder, manslaughter, firearms and explosives violations and other offences that might be associated with political violence). Juries are not used in Diplock courts; rather, one judge hears the evidence and determines whether to acquit or to convict the defendant. The court procedures also differ in Diplock courts. For example, a defendant cannot cross-examine a member of the police or British Army who testifies for the prosecution. The conviction rate in Diplock courts has been extremely high and this rate has been influenced greatly by the large number of signed confessions obtained from defendants while in police custody. Additionally, the high conviction rate has resulted in substantial increases in the prison population in Northern Ireland (Coogan 1996).

6. The MacBride Principles were named for Sean MacBride, former chief of Staff of the IRA, activist and co-founder of Amnesty International. As of October 1998, 16 states and 30 cities had passed legislation, endorsing the Principles. Also, federal legislation passed in 1998 requires that US companies in Northern Ireland follow the MacBride Principles if they hope to secure funding from the International Fund for Ireland.

7. A copy of the letter is in the author's possession.

8. Joseph Kennedy has provided other support to Nationalists in the north. For example, in the 1990s he wrote letters of protest to Prime Minister Tony Blair for his decision that in effect allowed the Orange Order to march down Garvaghy Road. His cousin John F. Kennedy Jr attended the funeral of Paddy Kelly, imprisoned since 1993. Kelly died of skin cancer just months after he had been transferred to the south of Ireland to complete his sentence. Some reports indicated, however, that Kennedy's attendance was for journalistic rather than political purposes. Another cousin, Mary Courtney Kennedy, married Paul Hill in 1993. Hill was one of the Guildford Four, released after the conviction was overturned but only after spending several years in an English prison. On the surface, then, it appears that at least

some members of this Kennedy generation are sensitive to and concerned about issues relating to the north of Ireland.

9. The pub has been raided on occasions since that time.

10. The testimonial bulletin that was distributed to persons who attended the dinner contained several support advertisements purchased by 39 businesses, 29 friends and acquaintances (some anonymous), 12 taverns and restaurants, four attorneys, two dentists and others. Not to be excluded was an advert purchased by members of the Gildernew Dart Team.

11. In an earlier case, former prisoner Sean Mackin was provided with adjustment of status (as opposed to political asylum) and granted permanent residency. In effect, deportation proceedings ruled in Mackin's favour. Bruce Morrison reported: 'No one has been able to describe legally how it happened' (correspondence with author). Some have suggested, however, that the death of Liam Ryan actually helped Mackin and a few others in their quest to have deportation proceedings dropped (Wilson 1995, p. 233n). As noted previously, Liam Ryan was a naturalised US citizen who upon returning to his native Ireland was assassinated by loyalist paramilitaries. That event may have provided Mackin with the evidence he needed to demonstrate a well-founded fear of persecution had he been returned to Ireland.

Chapter 3

1. Connolly (1985) reported that extradition proceedings were initiated just as Mackin was ready to board a plane for the south of Ireland.

2. Since the south of Ireland recognised citizens from north and south, theoretically that government could not have turned down Mackin's request.

3. Paul O'Dwyer emigrated from Ireland to the United States in 1925 where he became a well-known and respected defence lawyer. He worked on several cases involving Irish republicans in the United States. He is also noted however, for his proactive support for civil rights, an interest that spanned several decades. When several churches were destroyed by arsonists in the 1990s, his New York firm organised a fundraiser to help defray the costs of rebuilding, expenses that would otherwise have been paid solely by the African American church members. O'Dwyer, along with

Bernadette Devlin McAliskey, have been Irish activists and have also been most vocal in their efforts to support persons of other (non-Irish) backgrounds who face discrimination and persecution. Paul O'Dwyer died in 1998 at the age of 91.

4. Quinn was initially charged with other offences in addition to the murder of the police officer. However, the other offences were excluded from the extradition request by the British government.

5. Similar reasoning was used by the INS and the Bureau of Immigration Appeals (BIA) in deportation proceedings against Michael O'Rourke where the political offence exception did not apply because 'There is no war or rebellion in the Republic of Ireland' (United States Senate 1984, p. 59). The reasoning in both cases reflects either a general ignorance of the Irish conflict or provides justification for US judiciary in reaching the decisions.

6. The judge believed that the uprising did extend to England but believed that the case should have been returned to the District Court for a ruling to determine '...whether Quinn should be treated as an Irish National and afforded the protection of the political offense exception' (Ninth Circuit 1986, p. 821).

7. Barr's extradition hearing was held before the passage of the Supplementary Treaty.

8. Joseph Doherty, Desmond Mackin and Peter McMullen (first extradition warrant) all succeeded in fighting extradition; William (Liam) Quinn was unsuccessful.

9. The Anglo-Irish Agreement, established in November 1985 provided the south of Ireland with an advisory role in selected Northern Ireland affairs. As Metress (1995) noted, however, that role was quite limited but gave outsiders the impression that something was being done about the conflict. The US government backed the Agreement, a section of which established cross-border co-operation in the area of security, a move designed to 'severely hamper IRA operations' (Wilson 1995, p. 250).

10. Reagan had other reasons (also related to foreign policy) to target IRA members; he despised Colonel Gadaffi – and Gadaffi had allegedly supplied weapons to the IRA (Dillon 1992).

11. Scheduled offences are acts which are listed in a schedule or appendix to the Emergency legislation in the north of Ireland and are offences which are associated with the British *legal* definition of 'terrorism'. Legal proceedings differ for persons charged, arrested and convicted of

scheduled offences than for persons charged with 'ordinary crimes.' Although the British government strongly disputes the political motivation of republican and loyalist prisoners, Section 66 of the Emergency Provision Act 1991 as amended defines terrorism as the 'use of violence for political ends'.

12. Joseph Doherty was released from Long Kesh prison in November 1998 as part of the prisoner release scheme of the Good Friday Agreement.

13. After Jimmy Smyth was extradited some US supporters referred to the group as the H-Block 3. In turn, minor disagreement surfaced among US supporters over the name.

14. Several organisations were permitted to submit amicus briefs on behalf of Joe Doherty.

15. Extradition costs are supposed to be paid by the country that makes the request, regardless of whether extradition occurs. Under the Freedom of Information Act, I submitted a request to the Justice Department asking for the amount of funds paid to the United States by the British government in Jimmy Smyth's extradition case. No data/information could be located; expenses were not submitted to the British government. The US government paid the costs associated with Smyth's extradition using the taxpayers' money.

16. Following his extradition, Jimmy Smyth served just over two years in Long Kesh before being released in October 1998.

17. During this time, the British government practised the policy of 'internment' whereby nationalists were detained without charge for considerable lengths of time. The policy has a long history in Ireland but this phase commenced on 9 August 1971 when over 300 nationalists were seized by the security forces, placed in special 'camps' where they were held without charge or trial often for months at a time. Hundreds of other nationalists were taken by security forces and held in the months that followed.

18. 'Teachta Dála' (TD) is an elected member of the Irish (south) Parliament.

19. The Irish court granted extradition in November 1997. Kelly has appealed.

20. Mackin, McMullen and Doherty succeeded in fighting extradition under the 1977 Treaty with Britain. However, as mentioned earlier in this chapter, Mackin and Doherty were subsequently deported and McMullen was extradited under the 1986 Treaty after a second warrant was issued.

Chapter 4

1. Michael Flannery, displeased with the 1994 IRA ceasefire, became a vocal supporter of Republican Sinn Féin (as did George Harrison). Flannery died in 1994.
2. John Crawley, a former US marine, was born in the United States but spent part of his childhood in Dublin. Crawley served 11 years in Portlaoise prison for his role in the weaponry shipment. Upon his release from prison, he was allegedly part of an IRA unit that was sent to London after the collapse of the IRA ceasefire in 1996. He and other members of the unit were accused of planning to bomb a number of electrical power stations in England. Police searched the contents of more than 7,000 garages but never found any explosives. The defendants argued that their efforts were to serve as 'a hoax...in order to make the authorities shut down power themselves' (Hoge 1997); the actual placement of detonators and explosives and the intent to damage the power stations were not part of the plan (*Irish News* 1997c). Nevertheless, six of the defendants were convicted, including John Crawley who was sentenced to 35 years for conspiring to blow up the London electricity plants. In Janaury 1998, Crawley was transferred from an English prison to Portlaoise prison to complete his sentence.
3. Chuck Malone is also reputed to have vouched for William Quinn in his quest to join the IRA (see Chapter 3). Before his death in 1998 Chuck Malone had become an active supporter of Republican Sinn Féin.
4. The Stinger missile has a range of about three miles and is effective against low-flying aircraft such as British army helicopters used in the north of Ireland.
5. Entrapment is a legal defence to a crime in the United States; in essence, defendants admit to the crime but claim to have committed the crime only after strong encouragement, generally from law enforcement officers or informants.
6. For Irish republicans from Ireland, imprisonment in the United States differs substantially from incarceration in the north of Ireland. Republican prisoners in the United States are too few in number and are too often segregated to experience the political and cultural camaraderie that characterises republican subcultures in British prisons. Shared belief systems regarding the Irish struggle and the knowledge of common goals as part of that struggle in one sense makes it easier to serve time in the north of Ireland than elsewhere. Most other prisoners in the United States

generally do not understand, let alone share, the republican ideology and aspects of Irish culture are noticeably absent in US prisons.

7. The United States government made some attempts to pursue McGeough in Sweden where he resided for a time after leaving the United States.

8. The extradition and subsequent imprisonment of McGeough served to highlight the political milieu in the north of Ireland, for McGeough was a prolific writer. Like Joe Doherty, McGeough provided weekly columns about Irish politics and history for the *Irish People*. Peter Taylor (1997, p. 37) described McGeough as one who 'lives and breathes history'. He recalls dates and geographical settings of age-old events that have occurred in various countries. He speaks of world politics as if they are everyday topics of conversation. At the time of our initial interview, it had been 14 years since he had last lived in Ireland. Writing in prison is difficult. A prison environment is chaotic and characterised by loud chatter, music and other noise, a setting hardly conducive for the intensive thinking that is required for effective writing. The tools of the contemporary writer, the personal computer, library materials and other resources, are quite limited. Work space, in which to organise papers and notes, is at a premium. Concentration was bound to be affected yet he continued to write, at times rising at midnight and writing until the early hours of the morning. He noted that prison conditions in Germany were far worse than those in the United States yet he was more productive during his incarceration in Germany, which he reasoned was due to 'long periods of solitude'.

9. McNaught did, however, receive support from some fairly influential Irish Americans. This support took the form of letter writing, legal analysis and visits during his prison stay.

10. Police officers from various countries have received training at the FBI academy.

11. British government officials have also used war terminology to describe the political conflict in the north of Ireland. For example, Northern Ireland Secretary of State, Mo Mowlam, publicly announced in 1998 that 'the war is certainly over' (Anderson 1998).

Chapter 5

1. Mainstream media in this sense refers to the traditional sources that report general news. Mainstream media do not

include, for example, newspapers such as the *Irish Echo* and the *Irish Voice*, which cater generally to Irish and Irish American readers.

2. O'Hanlon (1998b) noted a few exceptions: journalists Pete Hamill and Jimmy Breslin have visited the north of Ireland and written from that perspective. Also, the *Christian Science Monitor* was one of the few news sources to have a correspondent based in Ireland. More recently Kevin Cullen, of the *Boston Globe*, was assigned to Ireland in 1997 for the purpose of establishing a full-time bureau. Added to the list of exceptions could be Jack McKinney who writes for the *Philadelphia Inquirer*.

3. 'Derry' was the original name of the city. The term 'Londonderry' was bestowed on the city by the British and so named for the London companies which exerted control in the area (Curtis 1984).

4. Censorship also occurs through the banning of books by the British government. Recently, Sean McPhilemy's book, *The Committee: Political Assassination in Northern Ireland* (1998), was banned in Northern Ireland and in Britain, although copies can be purchased through the Internet (Amazon withdrew the title from its British venue in June 1999 due to the threat of libel). In 1999 the Ministry of Defence banned *Ten Thirty Three*, a book written by journalist Nicholas Davies. The book was banned because it contained information and allegations about Brian Nelson, an alleged double agent for the British Army. Ironically, the ban on books may actually work to increase sales; *The Committee* made the *New York Times'* best sellers' list in 1998 (Martin-Clarke 1998).

5. The Good Friday Agreement is how the Belfast Agreement reached at the multi-party negotiations on Friday, 10 April 1998 has come to be known.

6. The Mitchell Principles were developed by US Senator George Mitchell, chair of the 'peace' talks, General John de Chastelain, former Canadian defence chief and Harri Holkeri, former Finnish Prime Minister. Among other issues, the Principles espouse non-violence. Elected representatives from political parties who wished to participate in the talks process were required to agree to the six principles.

7. Perhaps more controversial is the argument that suggests that the police depend greatly on the continuation of IRA violence. The number of police officers per capita indicates that the RUC is one of the largest police agencies in all of Europe. How can the government justify its policing expen-

ditures in a post-conflict situation? Hollywood (1997) suggested that during the 1994–96 IRA ceasefire the RUC helped to create the perception of a 'drug problem' in Northern Ireland in order to justify and indeed, in some areas, strengthen their numbers.

8. A subsequent 'hit list' consisting of the names and details of 150 people was found in the possession of loyalists in February 1999. The police waited nearly three months before notifying people whose names appeared on the list, a delay that created considerable controversy (Turner 1999).

9. For instance, the British government failed to initiate a thorough investigation into the 1989 murder of Belfast solicitor Pat Finucane. Nine years after his death, the United Nations appealed to the British government requesting an independent inquiry (Turner 1998). In other cases, victims' families, with assistance from a former judge from the United States and outside observers, have conducted public inquiries into the murders of their family members.

10. The killing of Diarmuid O'Neill in England in 1996 is but one of several examples. O'Neill was shot at least six times after police raided the residence in which he was staying. He was unarmed. Police were unable to locate guns or explosives on O'Neill's person or in the dwelling (American Protestants for Truth About Ireland 1996). After he was shot, O'Neill was dragged down the stairs and outside, where he received brief but unsuccessful medical attention. This action by the police led others to ask why O'Neill was not administered first aid in the residence and also, why he was moved at all.

11. Terry Enright had married a niece of Gerry Adams.

12. The horrific story of the three Quinn brothers reached an international audience.

13. Aogán Mulcahy (1995) examined news coverage of the 1981 hunger strikes. He found that of the ten hunger strikers who starved to death in order to gain political prisoner status, only one, Bobby Sands, was addressed in detail by the *New York Times*. The other nine were mentioned but remained nameless.

Chapter 6

1. A set of guidelines designed to promote equality in employment for US companies in the north of Ireland. The campaign for legislation commenced in 1984 and was

spearheaded by Father Sean McManus. The principles are named after Sean MacBride, Nobel Peace Prize recipient and co-founder of Amnesty International. MacBride also was a former member of the IRA for which he served as chief of staff (see also Chapter 2).

2. Supportive testimony was provided by congressional members Ben Gilman, Peter King, Tom Manton, Carolyn McCarthy, Robert Menendez and Richard Neal, among others.
3. For example, Adams was denied a visitor visa in 1984 by former President Reagan.
4. Candidate Dole did not appear to understand the many issues related to the north of Ireland. For example, in September 1996 he claimed to support a 'united Ireland' but later retracted the statement when he realised his 'error' (Mac an Bhaird 1996).
5. The killing of Dermot McShane is being considered by the European Commission of Human Rights.
6. See note 5, Chapter 2.
7. Some form of the designation had been in place at least since the 1970s (see Eilberg and Fish 1979).
8. Legal experts expect the terrorist law and its implications to be ruled unconstitutional (Smith, R. Jeffrey 1997).
9. As noted in Chapter 4, the Transfer Act has had little impact on Irish republican prisoners in the United States. Additionally, prisoners who are transferred to the north of Ireland from the United States are *not* entitled to early release.

Chapter 7

1. Written permission for fair use of lyrics was obtained from the songwriter, Kirk M. Olson.
2. The Northern Ireland (Emergency Provisions) Act has been amended on several occasions since 1973.
3. In previous years, some republicans had 'flirted with left-wing politics' although these efforts tended to reflect the views espoused by 'radical sections of the middle classes' (Ryan 1994, p. 51).
4. Shortly after the ceasefire ended, an acquaintance in Florida received her copy of the *Irish People* at her work address. The newsletter caters to Irish republicans in the United States. The copy had been defaced with the play on words: 'Get the Irish out of England.' In another example of vacillating support, the Irish Northern Aid chapter of south Florida had been scheduled to participate in the St Patrick's

Day parade. One week before the parade, the group was contacted and told that due to recent 'events' (that is, the end of the ceasefire) the group was no longer permitted to march.

5. Two of the families were dissatisfied with the documentary's contents, reporting that the television producer had altered the focus, containing information to which they would not have agreed (Scally 1998) but the deportation cases had nonetheless reached a very large audience.

6. On the surface it would appear that the British government has less influence upon deportation compared with extradition cases. However, British officials and RUC officers have testified in deportation cases. Several RUC officers, for example, testified during John McNicholl's deportation hearing in 1999.

Appendices

1. Research conducted by university faculty members in the US must be approved by a university human subjects committee (or the equivalent). The role of these committees is to ensure that ethical procedures (e.g., protection of respondents) are followed. I submitted a detailed research proposal to the University of Miami Human Subjects Committee and attended the Committee meeting at the time my proposal was being reviewed. The Committee decided that my research did *not* need its approval, i.e., that the risk to respondents would be minimal.

2. The assistance provided by jail officers stood in sharp contrast with visits to federal prisons. For instance, at one federal prison I waited with several other visitors in the prison parking lot when visits were delayed because of heavy fog. Even when the fog had lifted we were required to wait for approximately two hours before prison officials allowed us to enter the facility. During the waiting period, I conversed with several other visitors, many of whom were family members who had driven all night for the visit, only to witness the visit length dwindle (visitation periods are not extended even when visitors are delayed from entering the prison through no fault of their own).

3. The Department of Sociology, University of Miami, funded one trip to South Bend, Indiana, so that I could attend a conference at Notre Dame University at which several contacts were made. I am grateful for this support.

Name Index

Subject Index